P9-CKX-931

✳ Diseases

Volume 5

Infants and disease to Multiple sclerosis

Diseases

Volume 5

Infants and disease to Multiple sclerosis

Bryan Bunch
Editor

SCIENTIFIC PUBLISHING

GROLIER EDUCATIONAL

Editor: Bryan Bunch

Design and production: pam forde graphics

Writers:	*Illustrators:*
Barbara Branca	Jean Cassels/ Publishers' Graphics, Inc.
Bryan Bunch	Leslie Dunlap/ Publishers' Graphics, Inc.
Barbara A. Darga	Pamela Johnson/ Publishers' Graphics, Inc.
Betsy Feist	Kathie Kelleher/ Publishers' Graphics, Inc.
Gene R. Hawes	Joel Snyder/ Publishers' Graphics, Inc.
Wendy B. Murphy	
Karin L. Rhines	
Jenny Tesar	*Copyediting and index:*
Bruce Wetterau	Felice Levy, AEIOU, Inc.
Gray Williams	

Library of Congress Cataloging in Publication Data

Main entry under title:
Diseases.
v.<   >;cm.
Includes bibliographical references and index.
Summary: Alphabetically arranged articles present medical information on more than 400 diseases, discussing sources, symptoms, stages of the disease, its likelihood of striking, treatments, prevention, and long-term effects.
ISBN 0-7172-7617-1
1. Diseases--Encyclopedias, Juvenile.   [1. Diseases--Encyclopedias.]
I. Grolier Educational Corporation.
R130.5 D57   1996
616'.003--dc20   96-27606
                                                                    CIP
                                                                    AC

First published in the United States in 1997 by
Grolier Educational, Sherman Turnpike, Danbury,CT 06816

COPYRIGHT © 1997 BY SCIENTIFIC PUBLISHING, INC.

A HUDSON GROUP BOOK

✳ A newborn baby's cry may signal discomfort, hunger, or illness. However, infants are born with a certain amount of protection from disease that carries through the first year of life. This protection is passed from a mother to her child during pregnancy, and then after birth, through breast milk. Called *passive immunity,* this protection comes from the natural transmission of *antibodies,* chemicals that fight specific disease organisms. Passive immunity in infants helps prevent illnesses from occurring and shortens the course of a disease if it does occur.

Why infants respond to disease differently: There are many diseases that people of any age can acquire. However, because of their small size infants have the added potential of experiencing serious complications from diseases. For example, a common stomach "flu" (*gastroenteritis*) caused by a virus usually brings symptoms such as diarrhea and/or vomiting in both adults and infants. But in infants these symptoms can more easily lead to the potentially life-threatening problem of loss of bodily fluids or *dehydration.* An adult or older child is less likely to experience dehydration as quickly as an infant.

Most serious diseases of infants are caused not by viruses but by *bacteria.* A bacterial infection is usually treated with an medication known as an *antibiotic.* Frequently a physician will prescribe an antibiotic for an infant if a bacterial infection is merely suspected. The reason is that bacteria grow and spread rapidly in an infant's body. The earlier the medication is started, the more effective it is in killing the bacteria. Saving time and discomfort while waiting for laboratory test results is a good reason for starting treatment before diagnosis is confirmed.

How a physician determines cause of disease: When an infant is showing disease symptoms, he or she may be brought to a specialist in children's diseases, a *pediatrician* who will perform an examination. The physician will look over the entire little body, especially the mouth, eyes, nose, and ears, as well as press on, or *palpate,* the abdomen looking for confirming signs of disease. Questions about how the baby has been acting and eating usually provide further information to help determine the cause of illness.

When an infection is suspected, the physician may run a series of tests including blood and urine samples, X rays, and a culture from the location suspected to include some of the disease-causing microorganisms. (A culture is a sample of body tissues that is placed on a material that promotes growth of bacteria; the bacteria are said to be *cultured*.) For example, if the physician suspects a disease such as *meningitis,* a spinal tap would be performed to obtain the fluids that bathe and protect the spine and brain. Similarly, for a sore throat the culture would be taken from the back of the mouth.

If a heriditary disease is suspected, that is, one that has been inherited from parents, family history of disease is usually discussed. Many times parents are aware of the possibility of an infant inheriting such a disease and have been prepared through *genetic counseling*—advice from a trained person on how best to handle a possible genetic disorder.

Types of infant diseases and causes

Infectious diseases
Bacterial infections
Conjunctivitis (also viral)
Diphtheria
Otitis media (also viral)
Pertussis
Pneumonia (also viral or fungal)
Scarlet fever
Staph infection
Tonsillitis
Viral infections
Chicken pox
Conjunctivitis (also bacterial)
Croup
"German" measles (rubella)
Measles (rubeola)
Mumps
Otitis media (also bacterial)
Pneumonia (also bacterial or fungal)
Smallpox (no longer exists in the wild)
Fungal infections
Candidiasis
Pneumonia (also bacterial or viral)

Congenital diseases (genetic or developmental)
Autism
Cystic fibrosis
Down's syndrome
Hernias
Intussusception
Neural tube defects
Patent ductus arteriosus
SCID (severe combined immunity deficiency)
Spina bifida

Environmental diseases
Fetal alcohol syndrome
Lead poisoning
Rickets

Parasitic diseases
Lice
Pinworms
Scabies

Idiopathic diseases (of unknown cause)
Cradle cap
Guillain-Barré syndrome
Sudden infant death syndrome (SIDS)

Types and treatments of infant diseases: Some general concepts can be used in understanding infant diseases. For more specific information, see the entries on individual diseases or disease types.

Infectious disease: Infections are caused by microscopic organisms that invade an infant's body and quickly begin to multiply. When the body's immune system recognizes these foreign bodies, it begins to fight against the invasion by producing an army of immune cells called antibodies. Antibodies are chemicals produced by a kind of white blood cell. As blood rushes to the scene of the infection, the added blood causes the infection to look red. This immune response also increases the infant's body heat, causing a higher body temperature or *fever*. Sometimes infants "spike" a very high temperature, an event that does not commonly happen to older children or adults. As the antibodies destroy the microorganisms, the infection is reduced and eventually healed.

The major causes of infectious diseases in infants are bacteria, viruses, and fungi. Bacteria, which live and grow naturally in and on the human body, can increase in number to the point of causing an infection. Some produce poisons or toxins within the body that cause disease symptoms. Bacteria enter the infant's body in a variety of ways: by droplets released by a sneeze or cough that are breathed into the respiratory system; by ingestion into the digestive system; by blood transfusion into the circulatory system; or through a break in the skin. In general, bacterial infections are treated with antibiotics.

Viruses are not normally found within the body without causing an infection. Viruses are the cause of most common childhood infectious diseases, many of which can be prevented by vaccination (see Vaccination and disease). Viruses, many times smaller than bacteria, are not alive until they take over normal, healthy, living cells. Once inside cells, viruses can produce disease symptoms. Some viral diseases can be treated with medicines known as antiviral agents, but viruses are completely unresponsive to antibiotics.

Viruses are the primary cause of respiratory infections in infants. Such infections are treated mainly to make the infant more comfortable, but the infant's immune system alone has to kill off the viruses. Like bacteria, viruses enter the body by droplets, ingestion, blood, or breaks in the skin.

Earache
Fetal alcohol syndrome
Fever
Fragile X syndrome
Fungus diseases
Gastroenteritis
Gaucher's disease
Genetic diseases
Genital herpes
"German" measles (rubella)
Gonorrhea
Guillain-Barré syndrome
Hemophilus influenzae type B
Hernias
Hydrocephalus
Jaundice
Kawasaki disease
Labyrinthitis
Lead poisoning
Leukemia
Lice
Lyme disease
Measles (rubeola)
Meningitis
Mumps
Parasites and disease
Patent ductus arteriosus
Pertussis
Phenylketonuria (PKU)
Pinworms
Pneumonia
Poliomyelitis ("polio")
Reye's syndrome
Ringworm
Roseola
Scarlet fever
SCID (severe combined immunity deficiency)
Sickle cell anemia
SIDS (sudden infant death syndrome)
Sore throat
Spina bifida
Sprue
Stomachache
Syphilis
Tay-Sachs syndrome
Thalassemia
Tonsillitis
Vaccination and disease
Viruses and disease
"Virus" infection
Wilson's disease

Funguses, plantlike organisms that include mushrooms, yeasts, and molds, are also a cause of disease in infants. There are about a hundred types of funguses that live and grow naturally in and on the human body, but only ten or so of those types are disease-producing in humans.

Funguses reproduce by tiny spores that are carried in air or water. If the spores of funguses are inhaled or enter the body through a break in the skin, they can take hold and cause infection. The most common fungal infection in infants is *candidiasis*, commonly called thrush. This infection is treated with antifungal medications that kill the fungus. Fungal infections can become serious and even life-threatening if they are not treated, as they can spread throughout the body.

Congenital and genetic diseases and disorders: Congenital diseases are those that are present from birth but not inherited. Frequently a congenital problem is termed an *anomaly*, a malformation or absence of a body part. These diseases or anomalies can have environmental, idiopathic (unknown), or genetic causes. Most congenital diseases are related directly to a problem with the infant's *anatomy*, a specific body part or organ. Examples of these conditions are congenital heart defects such as *patent ductus arteriosus* and spinal cord disease, or *spina bifida*. Other common congenital problems in infants are found in the digestive system. Before birth a baby receives all of his or her nutrition directly from the mother's body. Shortly after birth the newborn's own digestive system begins to function and symptoms start to surface.

With increased scientific knowledge and skilled physicians, many congenital diseases and anomalies can be surgically corrected. Infants are remarkably quick to recover after successful surgery. A growing number of surgeries are performed even before birth, while the baby is still inside the mother's uterus. Conditions requiring surgery are diagnosed using ultrasound techniques.

Among of the most frustrating diseases are those with unknown causes, called *idiopathic*. However, an idiopathic disease of today may have its cause and cure discovered tomorrow.

Environmental diseases: Substances in an infant's environment that may be inhaled or ingested may be poisonous or toxic to the infant's body. Lead poisoning, which greatly affects the growing nervous system, can occur when an infant ingests paint chips containing lead. Unsafe conditions that lead to environmental diseases can be avoided through legislation and the education of parents.

Parasitic infestations: Although rare parasites can live in or on an infant's body, these are often quickly noticed and removed in the course of the frequent care given to an infant. Danger exists if the parasite is carrying a disease that passes into the infant's bloodstream undetected. Parasitic infestations are more of a major health concern in other parts of the world than in the United States.

Preventing diseases in infants: Many diseases can be prevented if certain precautions are taken to keep both an infant's body and environment free of disease-causing agents. Infants are very susceptible to ingesting disease-causing organisms because they frequently put their hands, toys, and other objects into their mouths. To help prevent infectious disease, bodily cleanliness is key. Because microorganisms cannot be seen unaided, special care should be taken to washing the hands of both infants and their caregivers. Using handkerchiefs or tissues when sneezing or coughing, avoiding contact with infected bodily fluids, and properly cleaning or disposing of diapers can stop the spread of infection. Also, pediatricians recommend that infants be given vaccinations against many childhood diseases (see Vaccination and disease).

An infant's environment should be a clean and healthy one, free of potential environmental hazards. Insects or other potential disease-causing vermin should be prevented from coming in contact with an infant. Foods should be properly cooked and handled to prevent contamination with bacteria or parasitic organisms. In preparing infant formulas, precaution should be taken against using water that could be contaminated with disease-causing organisms or chemical toxins.

✳ *Inflammation* is a condition of an area of the skin or any other tissue that has become sore, swollen, reddened with excess blood, or possibly fevered due to infection or injury. It results from the reaction of the body's *immune system* to any damage or to an attack on body tissues—including burns, stings, cuts, freezing, sunburn, or allergies, as well as most bacterial or viral infections.

Inflammation

SYMPTOM

A systemic inflammatory response can affect much of the body. This response might occur, for example, in the case of any of several different viral diseases that are often grouped with influenza as "the flu"—the familiar symptoms include fever, stuffy nose, sore throat, nausea, headache, and aching joints and muscles. This combination of immune responses is often referred to as *flulike symptoms.*

Medical terms for inflammation nearly always end with the suffix *-itis.* For example, *appendicitis* is inflammation of the appendix and *gastritis* is inflammation of the stomach.

Effects: Any disease or injury brings on some inflammation. This results when certain white blood cells called *mast cells* flock to body tissues that are being damaged and release the chemical *histamine.* Histamine and various immune-system proteins carry out a number of functions. They stimulate greater blood flow to the damage, bringing redness and fever. They also cause nerve endings to signal pain and capillaries to ooze blood to produce swelling of the area. In addition, they attract more white blood cells and antibodies to the site. Some white blood cells called *phagocytes* help kill any invading bacteria. Others release chemicals that help rebuild injured tissue. As a result, inflammation often plays a beneficial role in the body's processes for self-healing.

However, inflammatory processes can prove harmful in some cases. Pus may form at the site of an infection. It consists of microbes killed by white blood cells and the white blood cells that have themselves died in killing the microbes. Pus usually escapes through the skin or other surface tissue and healing is completed. But if the pus remains, it blocks healing and can become enclosed in a tough sac to constitute an *abscess.* Infections that act slowly, such as *tuberculosis,* can cause the inflammatory process to foster fibrous tissue that itself kills adjacent healthy tissue. This can lead to chronic internal abscesses or surface ulcers or sores.

Potentially most harmful can be inflammatory processes that actively attack healthy functioning. This is the case with *rheumatoid arthritis* and other *autoimmune diseases.*

Treatment: Cleanliness of the affected area and rest typically represent proper treatment for mild inflammation, inasmuch as they are part of the body's normal healing processes.

Many nonprescription drugs can help relieve symptoms of inflammation. Among them are aspirin, ibuprofen, and naproxen (nonsteroid anti-inflammatory drugs) to reduce both inflammation and fever throughout the body; antihistamines and decongestants for allergies; and ointments and liquids to relieve pain or itching caused by inflammation of the skin.

Abscesses and severe or chronic inflammations should be treated by a doctor. So should rheumatoid arthritis and other autoimmune diseases. Medications for autoimmune diseases may include corticosteriods or nonsteroid anti-inflammatories.

Influenza

DISEASE

TYPE: INFECTIOUS (VIRAL)

See also
Animal diseases and humans
Epidemics
Fever
Gastroenteritis
Guillain-Barré syndrome
Inflammation
Nose and throat conditions
Vaccination and disease
Viruses and disease
"Virus" infection

✳ Popularly known as "the flu," and sometimes called grippe, *influenza* is a relatively common, temporarily debilitating, viral infection of the respiratory tract, primarily the lungs. Often, however, other viral diseases are also called "the flu," even though they are not, strictly speaking, influenza. A disease is influenza only if it is caused by one of the influenza viruses.

It helps somewhat to keep these diseases straight by using *influenza* when speaking of the disease caused by one of the influenza viruses and using "the flu" for unspecified viral diseases that produce flulike symptoms. These symptoms do not include nausea or diarrhea, which are indicative of gastroenteritis or dysentery, even though such diseases, when mild, are often called "stomach flu."

Influenza spreads easily from person to person, so it normally appears as an epidemic. There are also isolated cases of the disease. Influenza epidemics, for reasons that are unknown, nearly always occur during cold weather.

Cause: There are three main types of influenza virus, categorized as types A, B and C.

• *Type C* is the mildest. Once an individual has gone through a course of infection and recovery, he or she is likely to have enough antibodies in the blood to resist further type C infections for life.

• *Type B* is somewhat less stable, meaning it has the potential to change its shape and evade detection by the body's patrolling antibodies; consequently, type B can result in occasional mild reinfections.

• *Type A* influenza virus is highly unstable; it changes its form, or "drifts," as the phenomenon is termed by epidemiologists (EP-uh-DEE-mee-OL-uh-juhsts—physicians who study epidemics). These changes are sufficient to make the antibodies developed in response to previous infections irrelevant.

Incidence: Type A influenza virus poses an annual threat of infection to populations around the world. Because it has a long history of developing severe strains in some years, type A is watched closely by national and international surveillance systems, including the U.S. Department of Health's Centers for Disease Control and Prevention (CDC). Each summer, based on the most current data available, an influenza vaccine particular to the anticipated active strain or strains is developed and persons considered at particular risk—the elderly, those with immune disorders and other serious chronic conditions, and individuals who work in the health care field—are urged to get a protective shot. Persons who are allergic to eggs, however, should get the advice of their physician first, as the vaccine is grown in an egg-based medium. Shots are typically administered in early fall to allow six weeks for protection to develop.

A large part of the remainder of the population (that is, those who did not get shots)—about 20% by the CDC's estimates—become infected and recover in a week to ten days. Perhaps 1% of those people require hospitalization because of complications, mostly bacterial pneumonia. The annual period of greatest risk is December to March in the northern hemisphere. According to the CDC, the economic costs of influenza are also high. Depending on the severity of the epidemic in any year, from 15 million to 111 million workdays are lost to influenza annually in the United States, not to mention the costs in physician and hospital visits, medications, and lost productivity among persons who are either coming down with the disease or working at less than normal energy during the period of recovery.

Symptoms you are likely to notice: Although symptoms of influenza are variable in severity, the most classic influenza infections are characterized by chills, high fever, runny nose, scratchy throat, headache, muscle ache, and general fatigue and weakness. Secondary bacterial infections such as bronchitis, pneumonia, and ear infections are sometimes also seen. A seldom seen companion is Guillain-Barré syndrome, a rare form

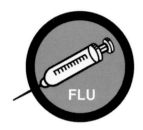

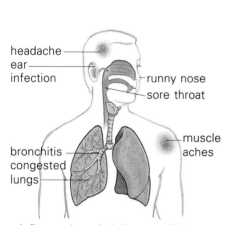

headache
ear infection
runny nose
sore throat
muscle aches
bronchitis
congested lungs

Influenza is a viral disease of the respiratory system, but the fight against the virus produces the symptoms we call "flulike"—headache, fever, fatigue, and muscle pain.

of damage to the nerves that causes muscle weakness in arms and legs. Guillain-Barré is apparently caused by an allergic reaction to the virus. Ironically, it is an equal-opportunity infection in that it may develop in reaction to an active influenza infection or to the killed influenza virus used to inoculate persons seeking protection from influenza.

Certain other diseases, such as the misnamed "stomach flu" (*gastroenteritis*), which may involve diarrhea and vomiting, are unrelated.

Treatment options: Influenza usually is self-limiting, and so is treated mainly with bed rest during times of high fever and a gradual return to activities as symptoms lessen in severity. The antiviral drugs amantadine and rimantadine often reduce the symptoms and shorten the length of the illness if given within 48 hours of onset of the symptoms. Antibiotics can be taken to treat secondary bacterial infections if they occur. None of the over-the-counter preparations, such as fever reducers and decongestants, affect the course of the attack, though they may make the sufferer feel more comfortable. It may not be desirable to reduce fever, however, as it is part of the immune process.

Stages and progress: After a brief incubation period of one to three days, there is a sudden onset of the main symptoms, often beginning with the combination of chills and fever—the patient may feel cold and shiver, but a thermometer will register a fever. Influenza is self-limiting and all symptoms are usually gone in about a week, although the length of illness can be as short as three days or as long as ten.

The main concern with most strains of the disease is that a secondary bacterial infection will set in while the body's immune system is taken up with fighting the virus. Such infections can be extremely dangerous in the young, the elderly, and those who are already weak from some other conditions, especially chronic lung diseases. Statistics concerning fatalities from influenza actually refer for the most part to such secondary infections.

History and pandemics: It is interesting to note that the origin of the disease's name, a corrupted form of the Italian word for "influence," comes from an early belief that it was provoked not by an infectious agent but by an *influentia coeli,* or celestial event. So sudden and severe was each epidemic that it seemed logical in a less scientific age to blame it on an extra-terrestrial event.

In addition to the annual patterns of drifts in the makeup of type A influenza strains, it is also known that major mutations, or shifts, occur every 10 to 40 years. These shifts, for which human populations have no immunity, result in *pandemics*, epidemics of global proportions. Nowadays these highly mutated influenza viruses may carry the name of a Chinese city or region as part of their identification (Asian flu, 1957–58; Hong Kong flu, 1968–69); this is because major mutations frequently make their first appearance on the Chinese part of the Asian mainland, where new strains of certain viruses common to barnyard swine readily make the leap to farming populations. Some think that domestic or wild ducks in Asia may also be incubators for new strains of the disease. New strains of influenza A may also carry numbered initials, indicating characteristic hemagglutinin (H) and neuraminidase (N) markers on the virus's surface.

Because influenza is an Old World disease, it ravaged the Native Americans after European contact in a particularly savage way. Native Americans had no immunity from earlier exposure to the disease. An epidemic that swept through the West Indies in 1493, soon after Columbus's first voyage, was probably influenza.

The great influenza pandemic of 1918

Before the behavior and origins of the virus were well understood, one of the most infamous of influenza pandemics struck the West in 1918. Called the "Spanish flu," in honor of the European country in which it was first noticed (although it was surely of Asian origin), it spread far and wide partly because of the movement of troops in World War I.

It is not surprising the World War I produced its own pandemic. War, especially on a large scale, provides a perfect setting for disease—large populations huddled together, rapid travel from place to place, shortages of food that weaken immune defenses, and wounded populations that are even weaker than the starving.

Influenza is a disease that occurs in pandemics on a regular basis whenever a new strain develops in its homeland of eastern Asia.

The influenza pandemic of 1917–18 was notable because the strain of the disease was especially deadly, killing the healthy as well as the infirm. For once influenza instead of secondary infections was the actual killer. Before the two-year-long pandemic was over it had infected an estimated 40% of the population in the United States alone and left as many as 500,000 Americans dead. Millions of people around the world died; more were killed by the influenza pandemic than by direct action in World War I.

✳ When a toenail curves under and grows into the tender skin of the toe, it can cause a lot of pain. This problem, called *ingrown toenail* since the nail grows into the toe instead of on top of it, can usually be avoided by good hygiene and well-fitting shoes.

See also
Foot problems

Causes: Ingrown toenails most often occur on big toes. They may result from an injury to the toe. More commonly, they are caused by cutting toenails down the sides in an elongated curve rather than straight across, parallel to the tip of the toe. Another common cause is wearing tight shoes that compress the toes.

Symptoms you are likely to notice: As an ingrown nail cuts into soft tissue around the top of the toe, you are likely to experience pain. An inflammation, with swelling and redness, may develop if the nail is attacked by the immune system. The sore place may become a site for infection.

Treatment options: Soak the foot in warm water to which you have added Epsom salts. This will relieve the pain and soften the nail and skin. Gently try to pull the skin away from the trapped edge of the nail. If successful, place a thin strip of cotton that has been soaked in castor oil between the skin and the edge of the nail. This will lift the nail slightly, preventing it from once again growing into the skin. Apply an antiseptic daily and keep the area clean and dry.

If the problem is severe or the area becomes infected, see your doctor. It may be necessary to perform a simple operation, using a local anesthetic, to remove the edge of the nail and some of the nearby skin. To combat infection, antibiotics may be prescribed.

Prevention: Trim your toenails on a regular basis. Cut toenails straight across using toenail clippers. Keep the outside edges of the nail longer than the middle if you have frequent problems. File the corners to eliminate sharp edges.

Wear comfortable, nonpointed shoes that provide plenty of room for the toes. Do not wear tight socks or pantyhose, which also can cramp the toes. Protect the toes against injury; for example, it is advisable to wear steel-toed boots if you lift a lot of heavy objects.

Insomnia

SYMPTOM

See also
Bipolar disorder
Clinical depression
Heartburn
Mental illnesses
Narcolepsy
Sleep apnea

✳ Everyone has a sleepless night from time to time. Lying awake night after night is another matter. With this condition, called *insomnia,* you do not get enough sleep to wake refreshed and able to function well during the day. Insomnia affects 25 million Americans all the time and millions of others some of the time. It strikes people of all ages.

Patterns of insomnia: Insomnia has different forms. Some people have trouble falling asleep. Others fall asleep easily but wake during the night and have trouble falling back asleep. Some people wake too early in the morning and cannot fall asleep again.

Of course not everyone needs the same amount of sleep. Sleep requirements normally decrease with age. Newborn babies sleep 18 hours a day, while teens need only 8 or 9 hours, and elderly people just 5 to 6 hours.

There are three types of insomnia:
- *Transient insomnia* lasts for several nights.
- *Short-term insomnia* lasts for 2 to 3 weeks.
- *Chronic insomnia* lasts for months or years.

Irregular sleep patterns are usually not a problem unless they are chronic and interfere with your daily life. If you are so tired during the day that you cannot concentrate, you may be prone to accidents. If you dread going to bed because you are afraid you will not fall asleep, your anxiety will keep you from sleeping.

Related symptoms: People with insomnia often complain of anxiety, depression, and irritability. Other symptoms may include mental confusion (*dementia*) and problems in concentrating and decision making. Insomnia also contributes to traffic and other accidents.

Insomnia may also be associated with other sleep-related disorders such as sleepwalking, sleep terrors, nightmares, and bed-wetting.

Associations: Insomnia is almost always a sign of another problem—either physical or emotional. Anxiety and depression are common causes of sleep loss. Stressful situations, such as losing a loved one, encountering money problems or job loss, travel, taking an exam, or giving a speech, can all lead to transient insomnia. Long-term insomnia is one of the main symptoms of serious depressive illness, including *clinical depression* and *bipolar disorder.*

The body cannot adjust quickly to abrupt changes in sleep schedules. These occur more often in a modern industrial society than they did in the hunting or agricultural societies of the past. A change in work shift—from working days to working nights, for example—is often a cause of insomnia. *Jet lag* is another source of sleep loss. In jet lag the internal body rhythms of those who fly long trips from west to east are upset. This upset often produces sleep disturbances.

Common physical causes of transitory sleep loss include *heartburn* and *restless leg syndrome.* Restless leg syndrome produces a crawling feeling inside the legs. These odd sensations force the affected person to get up and walk around until the feeling stops.

Insomnia in women sometimes appears during pregnancy or menopause, which is the life stage when a woman stops menstruating.

Two serious sleep-related disorders are sometimes related to insomnia: *sleep apnea* and *narcolepsy.* Sleep apnea is the sudden stoppage of breath during sleep. This seldom causes the person to awaken but disrupts normal sleep patterns, producing restless and unfulfilling sleep. Narcolepsy is a condition in which a person falls asleep several times a day for short periods. A person with narcolepsy may suddenly fall asleep even while talking, eating, or driving a car. Although this is quite the opposite of insomnia, any temporary insomnia from another source makes the narcoleptic attacks more frequent and prolonged.

Some other conditions, particularly *asthma, ulcers,* and the pain of *arthritis, migraine,* or *angina,* may cause interrupted sleep.

Prevention and possible actions: If insomnia leaves you feeling sleepy, tired, depressed, or anxious for three or more weeks, you should see your doctor for diagnosis and treatment.

Sleeping pills may help provide sounder sleep and improve alertness the following day. This relief is only temporary, since sleeping pills do not cure insomnia. For some types of insomnia, sleeping pills may be dangerous. The sleep that drugs produce is not natural or restful. After taking sleeping pills for a few days, you may feel more tired than ever and think that you need more of the drug. The more you use, the more disturbed your sleep. This creates a vicious cycle called *drug-dependent insomnia.* In one recent study, 40% of the people who complained of insomnia were dependent on the drugs they were taking to treat their insomnia. To prevent this, physicians seldom prescribe sleeping pills for more than three weeks. Nightly use is seldom advised. For stress-related insomnia, sleeping pills may be prescribed for only a few nights. In severe cases, a sleeping pill may be prescribed for a few weeks until psychotherapy takes effect.

Physicians do not recommend repeated use of over-the-counter sleeping pills because the long-term effects of their active ingredients are not known. Some may be habit forming for some people. Many drugs intended to induce sleep lose their effectiveness within two weeks if used regularly.

While alcohol relaxes some people enough to sleep, it leads to a shallow sleep with many awakenings. It is not a good idea to become dependent on alcohol to induce sleep. For one thing, regular use of alcohol at the same time each day is thought by some to contribute to the development of alcoholism. Furthermore, when alcohol is combined with sleeping pills, as often happens because of the shallow, unsatisfactory sleep induced by alcohol use, the result may be fatal.

Relief of symptoms: Remedies for insomnia include the following:
- regular exercise during the day, not at bedtime
- no caffeine-containing beverages after noon
- no smoking, since nicotine is a stimulant
- a hot bath or whirlpool before bed
- a glass of warm milk at bedtime
- no daytime naps
- reading a light book (no work-related material)
- a comfortable bed in a room that is neither too hot nor too cold
- counting sheep

Some sleep researchers recommend delaying bedtime for an hour or two if you cannot sleep. If you do not fall asleep within 20 minutes after trying this, get up and do some quiet activity, such as reading or working on a hobby. Do not smoke or eat. The next day, whether sleep came easily or not, get up at your regular time and try to get through the day without falling asleep. Do not let your days and nights get turned around.

Anything that relaxes, such as a warm bath, meditation, or reading in bed can help you get to sleep. Milk contains proteins that some find help sleep. A cool, but not cold, bedroom also contributes to sound sleep.

Sleep labs: wired for sleep

Over the past two decades researchers have opened a large number of "sleep laboratories" to study and treat sleep-related disorders. If you go to such a laboratory for a sleep-related problem, dime-sized sensors will be attached to your head and body. The sensors measure and record brain waves, muscle activity, arm and leg movements, and breathing. The physician uses this data about your sleep patterns to diagnose your problem and to prescribe a treatment tailored to your needs.

Treatments include relaxation techniques, yoga, and meditation. Biofeedback techniques are being used successfully in many labs. Bright-light therapy is sometimes employed.

✳ *Interstitial fibrosis* is one result of certain diseases and environmental exposures. Fibrous tissue not unlike a scar grows on the walls inside the lungs, which hold the air sacs essential to breathing—*interstitial* means "between the cells" in a medical context. The scarlike tissue, or fibrosis, cuts off more and more of the air sacs. In the most severe cases, death eventually results from lack of oxygen or heart failure.

Interstitial fibrosis that has no known origin is considered to be a disease in itself. In this rare disorder, not only is there the characteristic accumulation of fibrous tissue in the lungs, but also the terminal parts of the fingers, and occasionally the toes, become flattened. Nails curve around these "clubbed" fingers or toes and the cuticle seems to disappear. This form of interstitial fibrosis often progresses rapidly to respiratory failure and death.

Interstitial fibrosis
(in-ter-STISH-uhl fy-BROH-sis)

SYMPTOM

Associations: The symptom interstitial fibrosis is of perhaps widest interest in connection with today's worries over breathing asbestos particles released by fireproof insulation in older schools and homes. When disturbed by renovation or just deterioration over the years, asbestos from insulation can release tiny airborne fibers that can produce interstitial fibrosis. Large programs of replacing asbestos with less dangerous insulation in older school buildings have been carried out across the United States in recent years. Asbestos replacement is also widespread in homes and commercial buildings.

Interstitial fibrosis has a number of other causes besides asbestos particles, including inhalation of other small fibers or particles such as coal dust; silicon compounds, such as those produced by grinding and sanding; and fibers from textiles. The general name for lung diseases resulting from inhalation of harmful particles is *pneumoconiosis;* common names are based on the type of exposure (see Environment and disease).

Interstitial fibrosis can also develop from various diseases that cause inflammation of the lung or inhalation of irritating or corrosive substances.

Scleroderma, an autoimmune disease in which connective tissue turns rigid and hard, can also be a cause when it erupts on the inside wall of the lungs.

In the case of the specific disease called interstitial fibrosis, no cause has yet been located.

Treatment: Relief of symptoms and avoidance of the culpable irritant represent the main avenues of treatment for interstitial fibrosis. Limiting of physical activity can help cope with the shortness of breath that accompanies the condition.

Inadequate lung function can be compensated for by increasing the amount of oxygen breathed. Normally this is done in one of two ways.

• If a person is well enough to live at home instead of being hospitalized, he or she may keep a tank of pure oxygen and use it when needed or on a regular schedule. Ordinary air is only 20% oxygen, so breathing pure oxygen makes the oxygen five times as available to the damaged lungs as breathing air.

• If a person is hospitalized, he or she may be placed in an *oxygen tent,* an enclosed or partly enclosed region about the head within which the air is enriched with oxygen.

Prevention: Avoiding exposure to airborne particles of asbestos is probably the most important means of preventing this condition. Helping children escape from such exposure represents one of the main public health campaigns now under way across the United States. Workers in factories or mines that produce small particles or fibers need to follow work rules and wear masks when appropriate.

Intussusception

SYMPTOM

See also:
Digestive system
Diverticular diseases
Gangrene
Small intestine

✳ *Intussusception* is an alarming condition that develops without warning almost entirely in infants in their first or second year of life. It is a special type of obstruction of the intestine, nearly always of the small intestine. When it occurs, a part of the tubular-shaped intestine telescopes inside a neighboring part, like the finger of a glove that starts turning inside out while a glove is pulled off. Studies indicate it is contracted by fewer than 1 in every 500 infants. *When a child shows signs of having an attack of intussusception, he or she should be taken to a hospital as soon as possible.*

Symptoms you are likely to notice: Intussusception typically strikes without warning. In most cases, an infant having an attack feels acute abdominal pain that leads to screaming and drawing the knees up to the chest. The child usually vomits and turns pale as well. Attacks come periodically. Between them the child often calms and may seem to recover. Subsequent and still more severe attacks tend to bring straining to expel fecal matter, which will contain blood and mucus and thus resemble red jelly.

Symptoms your physician may observe: A physician might first note that the abdomen is swollen and hurts when touched even lightly. The physician also might feel the presence of a firm, rounded mass under the stomach wall on the upper right side.

Conclusive diagnosis is made with a barium enema. In this an enema containing the harmless chemical barium sulfate is given rectally, and an X ray of the intestinal tract is taken. The X ray clearly displays the intussusception.

Treatment: In addition to providing a definitive diagnosis, a barium enema itself succeeds in clearing up the intussusception of the intestine in some three out of every four cases that are free of complications. It is thought that the fluid pressure of the enema reverses the telescoped intestinal section causing the blockage.

Instances in which a barium enema fails to correct the condition usually require surgery. In such surgical operations, the intestine is manually manipulated to relieve the telescoping. This nearly always clears up the condition completely.

Should a part of the intestine have become too severely damaged by the condition to heal, the surgeon may remove the damaged section and connect the resulting ends together.

No certain causes have as yet been identified. Some cases seem to develop after recent infections, or at the site of a kind of polyp inside the intestine.

Prompt treatment is important not only to relieve acute pain but to prevent serious complications of later stages. These can include inflammation of the membrane enclosing all abdominal organs, puncture of the intestinal wall, and gangrene.

Irritable bowel syndrome

DISEASE

TYPE: UNKNOWN

See also:
Colitis
Crohn's disease
Diarrhea
Digestive system
Diverticular diseases
Gastroenteritis
Ileitis
Ileus
Large intestine

✳ Another name for the intestines is *bowels. Irritable bowel syndrome,* often called IBS, is a disorder of the large intestine that is marked by chronic distress—that is, the illness continues for a long period of time, generally for life. However, the problem is intermittent. People who have it experience bouts of either constipation or diarrhea, one after the other, but the symptoms mostly go away between outbreaks. The same person may experience constipation in some episodes and diarrhea at other times. Episodes of lower bowel irritation may also be accompanied by mild pain, slight swelling of the abdomen, and excessive digestive gas.

Irritable bowel syndrome does not lead those who have it to lose weight, to develop malnutrition, or to become prone to serious maladies of the digestive tract. Only in very rare cases does it seem to become so disabling that it interferes with a person's normal activities.

Other names for IBS used more often in the past have included spastic bowel, spastic colon, irritable colon syndrome, and functional bowel disease.

Incidence: Some reports indicate that IBS afflicts more than half of all patients who seek help from gastroenterologists, physicians who specialize in the digestive system.

About twice as many women as men develop IBS. Individuals of both sexes typically start to feel its effects in their adult years rather than as children.

Cause: Symptoms result from abnormal contractions, or spasms, of the smooth muscles of the colon that move food wastes through the large intestine. Some of these contractions may produce constipation, pain, and excessive gas. Others may result in attacks of diarrhea. No underlying cause of such abnormal action of the colon muscles has as yet been found.

IBS episodes often follow stressful incidents or emotional upsets. Stress is a common factor in many diseases. Some people react with skin outbreaks, others with stomach upset, some with heart palpitations, and still others with IBS.

Symptoms you are likely to notice: Digestive disturbances such as those characteristic of IBS are experienced by most persons at one time or another. These include constipation, diarrhea, stomachache, and excess gas, which on occasion produce acute discomfort. But what tends to distinguish IBS from such common digestive episodes is the recurrence of such signs, and the persistence of such recurrences year after year.

Further IBS symptoms may include a puffing-out of the abdomen, mucus with one's fecal matter, brief relief after passing much gas or having a bowel movement, and, even after a bowel movement, a feeling of not having emptied the bowel. Some persons with IBS have still more complaints that may include back pain, heartburn, constant fatigue, and faintness. Persons with IBS may find that their symptoms intensify after they have eaten certain types of foods, including cheeses, milk, and other dairy products, or foods producing undue amounts of digestive gas, such as cabbage.

Symptoms your physician may observe: Perhaps the most important determination made by a gastroenterologist or other physician in diagnosing IBS is to ascertain what it is not. Irritable bowel syndrome is sometimes deemed a disorder in normal digestive functioning and not classified as a disease. Physicians diagnose it by running tests that rule out diseases that produce symptoms resembling those of IBS. For effective treatment it is important to differentiate IBS from such diseases, which include *colon cancer, diverticulitis,* or inflammatory bowel diseases such as *Crohn's disease* or *ulcerative colitis.*

Tests might include lab analyses of feces and barium X rays of the lower digestive tract. They might also include a sigmoidoscopy, in which an instrument on a long thin tube is inserted through the anal opening up inside the colon. With this test, a physician can visually examine the inside walls of the intestine.

Negative results from all such tests combined with the patient's history of symptoms would typically lead to the diagnosis of IBS.

Treatment: An ongoing treatment program would likely be recommended by a physician once IBS has been diagnosed. Adjustments in diet are commonly called for. Increasing the amounts of high-fiber food in the diet relieves the effects of IBS in many cases. Among high-fiber foods are cereals and breads made with whole grains, vegetables, and fruits. If increased fiber in meals seems to be helping a patient, the doctor may also recommend using a high-fiber diet supplement available from pharmacies. Greater dietary fiber tends to be helpful if the person's IBS symptoms involve mainly constipation. Cutting back on or substituting for foods linked to outbreaks is essential.

Another aggravating factor may be eating large amounts of food during a meal. Switching to several small meals instead of two or three large ones may result in less discomfort from IBS.

Medicines prescribed may include antispasmodic drugs to help counter irregular contractions of the colon muscles. Laxatives on the one hand or antidiarrhea drugs on the other may be recommended in periods of special difficulty with constipation or diarrhea. However, doctors generally recommend use of these for limited periods of time only. Otherwise a patient may become overdependent on drugs to regulate bowel movements.

Psychological measures represent still a third type of remedy. Some persons with IBS have high anxiety levels that they seek to escape in vain by addictive smoking, drinking, or drugs. Reducing their anxiety through substance-abuse recovery programs and psychotherapy often improves their IBS condition. Self-help groups of people with IBS may be formed for group therapy. Individual counseling to reduce feelings of stress may also better the condition. Tranquilizers such as Valium may be prescribed to lessen anxiety or stress in some cases. Doctors recognize the tranquilizers as potentially habit-forming and usually have patients take them for limited time periods only.

✳ *Ischemia* is a condition in which any tissue or organ of the body fails to receive an adequate supply of blood. Its effects can range from only moderate discomfort to paralysis to fatality. Severe ischemia in some parts of the body can require immediate emergency action in order to save a life.

Ischemia of the brain may cause a *transient ischemic attack,* which has symptoms such as headaches, dizziness, tingling, numbness, blurred or double vision, or sudden weakness or partial paralysis of one side of the body. Such transient attacks require medical attention because they are often precursors of a more dangerous *stroke.*

Associations: Ischemia, or an insufficient blood supply, can affect any part of the body as a result of physical injuries that slash or crush arteries. An *aneurysm* that bursts results in ischemia for any tissues supplied by that particular artery.

The tissues of any part of the body die when deprived of blood. The amount of time it takes tissue to die varies from organ to organ, however. In cases of ischemia for any prolonged time, regardless of the cause, the chief concern is *gangrene.*

The experience of having a leg or an arm grow numb after having been held in a cramped position that reduces the blood supply—and having the limb tingle with "pins and needles" as blood circulation returns after the limb had "gone to sleep"— represents a familiar instance of very mild ischemia. Except in the case of wounds, blood supply is nearly always restored to skeletal muscles before any damage is done. The feeling of discomfort usually causes a person to move the part affected, thus restoring blood to the muscles. When an arm or leg is pinned into one position for a long time artificially, however, damage, including gangrene, can occur.

Another mild and easily remedied form of ischemia is familiar to anyone who has had *leg cramps* after heavy exertion with the leg muscles. An insufficient blood supply causes these cramps, which dissipate after a brief rest.

Ischemia in the brain or heart is especially serious. Brain tissue is particularly sensitive to blood supply. The brain or any part of it dies if deprived of blood for only four or five minutes. Heart tissue also dies in a matter of minutes if deprived of blood. By contrast, the kidneys can go on functioning without adequate blood for an hour or more.

Ischemia
(ih-SKEE-mee-uh)

SYMPTOM

See also
Aneurysm
Arteries
Circulatory system
Cramp
Gangrene
Heart attack
Heart failure
Hypertension
Kidney diseases
Kidneys
Leg cramps
Stroke

A *heart attack* is perhaps the most serious condition that can be precipitated by ischemia of the heart. Also very serious is *stroke* from ischemia in part of the brain. Strokes often paralyze parts of the body or impair other functions controlled by parts of the brain in which tissue has been killed by ischemia. Similarly, in heart attacks parts of the heart muscle that have been deprived of blood die. If extensive enough, either a heart attack or a stroke can be fatal.

Although the *kidneys* can last for a time without blood supply, complete ischemia of the kidneys soon leads to kidney failure, which is fatal if not treated. Similarly, other organs, such as intestines, deprived of blood may develop gangrene with fatal consequences.

Treatment: In general, restoring blood flow as quickly as possible resolves most ischemia. If the cells have died, it may be necessary to remove the affected region. In some cases, this may require amputation of a limb.

Emergency action at the first signs of either a heart attack or a stroke might save the life of a person giving evidence of either form of ischemia. Sudden, very sharp pain in the chest, and possibly also in a shoulder or arm, is perhaps the most common sign of a heart attack. Slurring of speech and paralysis—shown in such ways as loss of control of fingers or hand, limping or foot dragging, or drooping of the features on one side of the face—are common signs of the start of a stroke.

As soon as signs of heart attack or stroke are noticed, the victim should be gotten to a hospital emergency room immediately.

Prevention: The major preventive measures for ischemia are those often taken to avoid its most dangerous forms, which are heart attack and stroke. Among primary measures to prevent heart attacks (and the *hypertension* that can lead to them) are avoidance of foods high in cholesterol and saturated fats, sufficient regular exercise (especially aerobic), and weight reduction if needed. Hypertension can be controlled with medication if exercise and diet do not resolve the problem. For persons thought to be prone to having strokes, anticoagulants to forestall blood clots are recommended in some cases. A physician may suggest taking a low-dose aspirin daily, but such a step should be taken only on a physician's advice as aspirin can have powerful side effects.

✳ *Itching* is an annoying symptom of many different conditions. Self-diagnosis may be difficult because of this. Nevertheless home remedies or over-the-counter medications are usually effective. In some rare cases, itching is a sign of a serious illness. Severe itching is termed *pruritis* (proo-RY-tuhs) in medical terminology.

Parts affected: Itching affects many body parts, although it is always the skin or mucous membrane over those parts that actually itches. Itching is usually divided into two types: with a rash and without a rash (see Rashes).

Related symptoms: Many related symptoms accompany itching. The most common is a rash. Other symptoms include blisters, skin pain, fever, and skin flaking

Associations: Some common causes of itching are listed below:

• *Allergies* are a very common cause of itching. They also can cause rashes. Allergies to food, soaps, cosmetics, and prescription drugs often begin as an itch, then develop into a rash after you scratch them. Itching is often the first and sometimes the only sign of an allergy. A rash or hives may follow. Prescription drugs may cause an allergic reaction that includes itching.

• *Anal itching*, particularly common in children and older people, has many causes. It usually happens because fecal material is irritating nerve endings in the anus. Other possible causes include *pinworms, hemorrhoids, cracks in the skin surrounding the anus, anal warts,* or an *allergy to toilet paper.* Sometimes anal itching is a sign of a fungal infection, which in turn is an early sign of *diabetes mellitus.* In rare cases, it is a sign of an *abscess, polyps,* or a *sexually transmitted disease.*

• *Athlete's foot* is a fungal infection that causes cracks between the toes. These cracks itch and burn.

• *Dandruff* can be accompanied by itching. White flakes falling from the scalp and scalp itching are often signs of *seborrheic dermatitis,* a common yeast infection that inflames the skin of the scalp.

• *Genital itching*, often called *jock itch,* is most often caused by a fungal infection anywhere on the genitals. It may start as just a small patch of red but advance to serious inflammation. Other intense itching can be caused by *scabies* or *pubic lice.* In

Itching

SYMPTOM

See also
Allergies
Athlete's foot
Chicken pox
Eczema
Fungus diseases
"German" measles (rubella)
Hemorrhoids
Hepatitis A and E
Hepatitis B and similar diseases
Hives
Jaundice
Jock itch
Lice
Liver
Measles
Neuropathy
Pink eye
Pinworms
Poison ivy, oak, sumac
Psoriasis
Rashes
Ringworm
Scabies
Seborrhea
Sexually transmitted diseases (STD)
Shingles
Skin diseases
Stings
Sunburn

women genital itching, called *pruritis vulvae,* can be the first sign of a yeast infection. In both sexes, intense genital itching and pain can be the beginning of *herpes simplex type 2.*

- *Liver disorders* produce itching combined with *jaundice.*
- *Nerve irritation,* known as *neuropathy* or *neuritis,* often causes pain along with severe itching.
- *Pink eye* is the common name for a contagious infection that causes red eyes with a yellowish, crusty discharge. Usually the eyes itch, water, and burn with pink eye.
- *Poison ivy, oak,* and *sumac* are plants to which most people are allergic, so exposure to them causes a severe skin rash that itches intensely.
- *Ringworm* is a fungal disease that has itching as one symptom, often in the scalp.
- *Shingles,* also known as *herpes zoster,* is a viral nerve disease produced by the same virus that causes chicken pox. It almost always results in a rash along a long, thin area of the body, following a nerve, and burning or stabbing pain along with itching.
- *Skin diseases* often have itching as a symptom. These include *eczema, psoriasis,* and *seborrhea.*
- *Stings and bites,* especially mosquito or gnat bites, are the most common cause of itching, mostly as a result of a mild allergic reaction to the bite. Bee and wasp stings and bites from flies other than mosquitos and gnats cause more pain than itching, but they can also cause severe allergic reactions in some people.
- *Sunburn* can cause skin itching, especially when the burned area begins to peel or flake.
- *Viral diseases* that produce rashes or blisters, such as *chicken pox,* "*German*" *measles (rubella),* or *measles,* also induce itching, which can be severe in some instances, especially with chicken pox.

Prevention and possible actions: When bathing, use a mild soap or soap substitute to prevent skin irritation that causes itching. Pat yourself dry after bathing—do not rub your skin. Use a moisturizer after bathing to keep the skin from becoming too dry.

Women with sensitive skin should use antiallergenic makeup and shampoo. If you think that your skin may be sensitive, check for allergies to your cologne, aftershave, etc.

Itching can have many causes, but one rule always applies: Do not scratch.

Everyone with sensitive skin should avoid heat, direct sunlight, hot water, and overheating exercise. It also helps to wear loose cotton clothing; synthetics or wool can irritate the skin.

Insect bites can be prevented by using a repellent, especially one that contains DEET. It is better to apply repellents to clothing than directly to the skin.

Relief of symptoms: The most important way to get relief from itching is also the most difficult way—do not scratch! Instead use ice until the itch dies down. Sometimes a cool shower or cold compresses may help relieve the itch.

There are a number of over-the-counter medications that relieve itching. A well-known one is calamine lotion, which works best for blister itches, such as poison ivy. Oral antihistamines often help relieve allergy symptoms, including itching. Cortisone ointment is often used, but it is important to limit use to a day or two as cortisone will thin skin and lose effectiveness with prolonged use.

If over-the-counter medications do not work, a physician may prescribe more powerful antihistamines, ointment, or creams. Prescription antihistamines are usually recommended for use in chronic conditions. Pills that relieve itching for 24 hours at a time are now available, as well as more powerful ointments and creams for treatment of serious skin diseases.

If your itching is severe and lasts more than two days, and there is a family history of *diabetes* or *kidney disease,* or it is accompanied by the yellowish skin and eyeballs of *jaundice,* see your doctor.

Instead of scratching an itch, one way to make it feel better is to apply ice to the skin.

Jaundice is characterized by a yellowing of the skin and whites of the eyes. It is a signal to see a doctor. Something has interrupted the normal functioning of the liver, gallbladder, or blood. Babies, especially if premature, often show mild jaundice at birth; this normally clears up in a day or two.

Jaundice
(JAWN-dis)

SYMPTOM

Parts affected: When old red blood cells are broken down, an orange-yellow pigment called bilirubin is formed. The liver removes bilirubin from the blood and excretes it in bile. Bile is a fluid that is stored in the gallbladder, then discharged through biliary ducts into the small intestine, where it aids in the digestion of fats. If the amount of bilirubin builds up in the blood, the skin and whites of the eyes—which contain numerous small blood vessels—become yellowish.

Related symptoms: Jaundice is often marked by changes in the color of the urine and feces. The urine may darken to brownish green. The feces, which normally eliminate bilirubin from the body, may turn grayish. Itching and abdominal pain may also be present.

Associations: Jaundice may result from any of the forms of hepatitis or from cirrhosis or other liver disorders; in these diseases, the liver cells do not transfer bilirubin to bile, thus allowing bilirubin levels in the blood to build up. In obstructive jaundice, gallstones or a tumor on the pancreas blocks the bile (biliary) ducts; bile builds up in the liver and bilirubin is forced back into the blood. Sometimes newborns have jaundice as a result of a congenital obstruction of the bile ducts.

In *hemolytic jaundice*, there is an excessive breakdown (hemolysis) of red blood cells; more bilirubin is produced than can be processed by the liver. This process can sometimes come from an immune reaction of a baby to antibodies in its mother's blood, producing severe jaundice at birth.

Alcoholism and prolonged alcohol abuse often lead to a breakdown in liver function, resulting in jaundice. Certain drugs may produce jaundice as well.

Prevention and possible actions: The doctor will perform various tests to determine the cause of the jaundice. Blood tests and a liver biopsy may be needed if liver problems are suspected. Ultrasound may be used to locate blockages in the bile ducts. Bilirubin levels in the blood will be tested if hemolytic jaundice is suspected.

Relief of symptoms: Treatment will depend on the cause of the jaundice.

Jock itch

✳ *Jock itch* is a minor fungus disease that affects the area of the genitals—its name is short for jockstrap itch, which describes the region that is affected. Its typical symptoms include itching and the emergence of reddish, slightly swollen patches covered with flaky or scaly skin.

Jock itch develops most often in warm weather and is contracted mainly by boys and men. Its medical name is *tinea cruris.* Though it occurs in a different location, its symptoms resemble those of *athlete's foot,* another disease caused by funguses of the tinea group. Often a person will experience jock itch and athlete's foot at the same time.

In other locations, often the head in children, a tinea fungus is *ringworm.* Some call any of the tinea group ringworm.

Incidence: Jock itch occurs commonly among males. Some people are naturally more susceptible than others. Girls and women also develop jock itch, but appear to do so rarely.

Cause: Jock itch is not contracted from someone else, as is often the case with a bacterial or viral infection. The fungus causing jock itch is normally present on the skin. When the crotch area becomes warm, moist with sweat, and closed off from the outside air for long periods of time, the tinea fungus grows faster and attacks on the skin become noticeable.

Wearing tight underpants or pants or being heavily overweight also increases one's chances of developing jock itch. The fungus thrives in close places where conditions stay moist, which includes any place where two skin surfaces come together. These regions are larger in persons who are overweight.

Jock itch and other fungal skin infections often occur temporarily as a side effect of taking antibiotics. Normally the balance between harmless skin bacteria and tinea fungus prevents the fungus from multiplying extensively. Antibiotics can greatly reduce the number of bacteria, providing a situation in which the funguses can spread and become more dense. Jock itch caused by this mechanism usually clears up when antibiotic use has ceased and the skin bacteria return.

Males in whom it develops need not be concerned that it is one of the sexually transmitted diseases. Jock itch develops without any sexual contact whatever.

Girls and women should similarly be careful to differentiate a case of jock itch from *vaginitis.* Some forms of vaginitis, which bring itching and irritation of the vulva and vagina, are caused by funguses in the form of yeasts; these funguses differ from those that cause jock itch.

DISEASE

TYPE: INFECTIOUS (FUNGAL)

See also
Athlete's foot
Fungus diseases
Ringworm
Vaginitis

Treatment: Most cases of jock itch clear up by themselves. Cures can be speeded in mild cases by keeping the crotch area cool, dry, and clean, and by wearing loose clothing so that air can get to the affected area more easily. Traditionally the most common treatment was to apply powders that helped keep the affected region dry. In recent years, however, over-the-counter antifungal ointments, powders, and liquids have become available. These are all applied directly to portions of skin inflamed by jock itch. They are far more effective than simple powders.

Severe and persistent cases seldom arise. When over-the-counter treatment fails, however, one should be examined by a physician. A skin specialist can not only make certain that the itch is caused by tinea, but can also prescribe more powerful antifungal drugs if necessary.

Prevention: Jock itch can be discouraged by avoiding the conditions that cause it—such as abnormal heat, sweat, and tight clothing in the groin. It is helpful to attack the problem as soon as it starts, when the fungal involvement is still limited.

Kawasaki disease

(KAH-wuh-SAHK-ee)

DISEASE

TYPE: INFECTIOUS (BACTERIAL)

See also
Bacteria and disease
Immune system
Scarlet fever
"Staph"
"Strep"

✳ In recent years a number of apparently new diseases have appeared or been identified for the first time. Perhaps the most familiar are AIDS, Lyme disease, Legionnaire's disease, and Ebola.

One of the most mysterious of these apparently new ailments is *Kawasaki disease,* so named because it was first identified in 1967 by Tokyo pediatrician Tomisaku Kawasaki. It is similar to *scarlet fever* and probably was often identified as such in the past. Another name used for this disease is *mucocutaneous lymph node syndrome* (MLNS), which describes its characteristic inflammation of the mucous membrane of the mouth and swollen lymph nodes.

Cause: Originally the cause of Kawasaki disease was completely unknown. Early in its short history it was attributed to a retrovirus (the type that includes the HIV virus), to allergies to dust mites, and to infection by various bacteria. In 1993 the disease was firmly tied to toxins produced by two different bacteria—a previously undiscovered strain of staphylococcus bacterium and a variety of streptococcus bacterium. The symptoms are produced by a combination of the immune system response to the bacteria and to the toxins they produce.

Scarlet fever, the near twin of Kawasaki, is similarly caused by a streptococcus bacterium and immune reactions. One difference is that there is no complication from staphylococcus.

Incidence: There are about 5,000 cases annually in the United States, and cases around the world as well. Like scarlet fever it tends to attack children, although the children that are the main victims of Kawasaki are most often younger than two. Although scarlet fever has become less common in recent decades, Kawasaki disease has been on the rise, possibly because of better diagnoses.

Symptoms you are likely to notice: Kawasaki disease is similar to scarlet fever in that the patient has a high fever followed by a rash that may include skin peeling off the arms and legs. The main identifying symptom is a rash on the tongue, known as strawberry tongue. The lymph nodes in the neck are generally swollen (commonly known as swollen glands).

The illness starts suddenly, with little distress before full onset of the symptoms.

Symptoms your physician may observe: The membranes of the mouth are seen to be inflamed when examined under good lighting.

Treatment options: Once the disease has been identified, it can be eliminated in most cases with a course of antibiotics. Treatment has often consisted of large doses of aspirin over long periods of time to reduce inflammation and help prevent heart complications.

Stages and progress: Kawasaki disease often produces symptoms common to those of many bacterial infections, including diarrhea, pneumonia, and ear infections, depending on which organs are invaded by the bacteria. Joint pain is common.

Like scarlet fever, it can produce heart disease as a complication, although the form of the heart disease—aneurysms of the coronary arteries—is different from the valve disorders that result from scarlet fever.

Risk factors: Unlike most infectious diseases, Kawasaki disease does not seem to spread easily from person to person. Therefore scientists suspect that something in the genetic makeup of a victim causes the immune system to react to the bacterial invasion differently. One person may overcome the disease or have mild symptoms, while a small child with a poorly developed immune system and perhaps a tendency toward the disease may become very ill.

There are no specific steps one can take to prevent the disease, but watching for the symptoms and getting appropriate treatment early can prevent complications from developing.

Kidney and bladder stones

DISEASE

TYPE: CHEMICAL
        MECHANICAL

See also
Colic
Excretory system
Gout
Kidneys

✳ *Kidney and bladder stones* can take years to form and during that time may produce no symptoms. Small kidney stones may even pass harmlessly out of the body by way of the *ureter* (yuu-REE-tuhr), the tube connecting the kidney to the bladder. But as often happens with people who get kidney stones, a large stone can become stuck in the ureter. Then the patient suffers terrible pain until the stone finally passes, or until a physician breaks up the stone or surgically removes it.

Stones formed in the bladder tend to be larger than kidney stones and usually are symptoms of such underlying disorders as an enlarged prostate or urinary tract infection.

Cause: Stones usually begin forming in the kidney when the urine has become too concentrated. Various substances in the urine, such as calcium salts or uric acid, then begin crystallizing into small bits of hard material in the kidney. Over time the crystals grow in size until they become large enough to cause problems.

Four types of kidney stones are the most common.

• *Calcium stones* form when calcium and another substance, such as phosphate, crystallize in the urine. Foods rich in calcium, such as milk, and diseases of the small intestine may promote growth of these stones.

• *Uric acid stones* form when there is too much uric acid in the urine. People with *gout*—a common disorder caused by too much uric acid in the blood—account for about half the cases involving these stones.

• *Struvite stones* can develop as a complication of a urinary tract infection, usually in women. The stones can become very large.

- *Cystine* (SIS-teen) *stones* occur in the kidney and bladder and result from an inherited disorder called *cystinuria* (SIS-tih-NYUUR-ee-uh). Recent research has linked cystinuria to a genetic mutation on the second chromosome. With this disease the kidney fails to reabsorb enough of some amino acids, including the amino acid cystine that goes into forming the stones.

At least sometimes there is a genetic link with the other stones as well: The tendency to form kidney stones has been shown to run in families. A tumor on the parathyroid gland also causes stones to form, but this is a fairly rare circumstance.

Incidence: Kidney stones are relatively common and affect anywhere from 240,000 to 720,000 people in the United States each year. About 10% of men and 5% of women will have at least one kidney stone by the time they reach old age. Bladder stones by comparison are not very common and 95% of the cases occur in men.

People with urinary tract infections, those who have a history of certain intestinal problems, and those who are immobilized for extended periods all have a greater risk of forming kidney stones. Medical experts also note that people living in areas of high heat and humidity are more likely to have stones.

Calcium stones are by far the most common type, occurring in 75 to 85% of cases. Men are two to three times as likely as women to get calcium stones. Uric acid stones account for about 8% of all kidney stones. Struvite and cystine stones make up the balance.

Symptoms you are likely to notice: Kidney stones sometimes cause no symptoms at all, but when large enough to become stuck in the ureter, they cause a painful condition called *renal colic* (REE-nuhl COL-ik). The pain usually begins in the area near the kidney and gradually moves downward toward the groin. The pain comes in waves and can be very intense. Patients with renal colic may also experience a constant need to urinate and notice blood in their urine.

Bladder stones tend to become fairly large and so often cannot pass out of the bladder along with the urine. Patients with these stones experience a frequent urge to urinate, pain on urination, and possibly blood in the urine. They may also be unable to urinate except in certain positions.

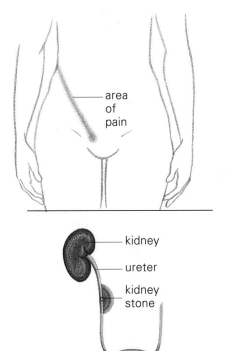

The path of pain of a kidney stone follows the ureter as the stone moves or tries to move into the bladder. The side on which the pain develops depends on which kidney is involved.

Symptoms your physician may observe: Because kidney stones may present no symptoms at all, they sometimes are discovered accidentally during routine X-ray examinations. If you have renal colic your physician will probably order blood and urine tests as well as an ultrasound scan to locate the stones. Another way to locate the stones, an *intravenous pyelogram* (PY-uh-loh-gram), is a series of X rays taken after you have been injected with a substance that highlights the various parts of the kidney. The stones do not show up on the X rays, but the injected substance flowing around them reveals where they are.

Treatment options: Surgery was once the only option when kidney stones became stuck in the ureter. In recent years, though, a procedure called *lithotripsy* (LITH-oh-TRIP-see) has largely replaced surgery. A machine called a *lithotripter* is used to focus shock waves on the stones, breaking them up to let them pass out of the body. Ultrasound may be used for stones that become stuck in the lower part of the ureter.

Medication can sometimes dissolve bladder stones. Surgeons may remove small bladder stones with a *cystoscope* (SIS-tuh-SKOHP), a tube that is inserted through the urethra, the duct that carries urine from the bladder out of the body. A form of lithotripsy is used to break up larger bladder stones.

Prevention: Drinking six to eight glasses of water a day is a basic measure for preventing recurrence all types of stones. The drug allopurinol helps block formation of uric acid and so can be used to prevent new uric acid stones. A different medication blocks the forming of new calcium stones. Clearing up a urinary tract infection quickly with antibiotics prevents the recurrence of struvite stones.

Kidney diseases

✳ Kidney diseases can be very serious because of the important role the kidneys play in removing excess fluids and wastes from the body. Infections of the kidney, kidney stones, inherited kidney disorders, and even cancerous tumors can all interfere with normal operation of the kidneys. Some of these diseases lead to permanent kidney damage and even death.

Among the major kidney diseases are the following:

• *Kidney infection,* also called *acute pyelonephritis* (PY-uh-loh-nih-FRY-tis), can arise from an untreated urinary tract infection. Infection often leads to more serious kidney problems and may be life-threatening to the elderly or someone in a weakened state.

• Inflammation of the kidney, *nephritis* (nih-FRY-tis), also known as *Bright's disease* and *glomerulonephritis* (GLOM-uh-rool-oh-nef-RY-tis), usually involves the small ducts in the kidney, the clusters of capillaries in the kidney, or the tissue between them. Acute nephritis sometimes produces few symptoms and with treatment recovery is usually complete. In a few cases the disease recurs and becomes chronic nephritis, which causes a progressive decline of renal function—*renal* (REE-nuhl) is the adjective physicians use to mean "of the kidneys."

• *Nephrotic* (nuh-FROT-ik) *syndrome,* which sometimes attacks young children, is characterized by high levels of protein in the urine and by swelling around the eyes and abdomen. It can lead to chronic nephritis.

• Inherited kidney disorders include *polycystic* (POL-ee-SIS-tik) *kidney disease* and *cystinuria* (SIS-tih-NYUUR-ee-uh). Polycystic kidney disease, which affects about 400,000 adults, causes clusters of cysts to form on the kidney. With cystinuria tubules in the kidney fail to reabsorb enough of some amino acids (including cystine), allowing the amino acids to be excreted in the urine. This leads to the formation of kidney and bladder stones (see Kidney and bladder stones).

• Inherited abnormalities of a valve in the tube leading from the kidney to the bladder causes *reflux,* the most common urinary tract problem found in children. In this disorder urine flows backward from the bladder up into the kidney. This damages the kidney by creating abnormal pressure and increasing the likelihood of kidney infections.

Causes: Kidney function can be impaired or lost in a number of ways. Infections and other disorders such as those mentioned above may be brought on by urinary tract infections, allergic reactions to drugs, or even the body's own antibodies that have been produced to fight off an infectious disease like streptococcal infection, pneumonia, or typhoid fever. A *tumor* may also affect kidney function (see Cancers). Rare inherited kidney disorders not mentioned above also exist.

Serious problems with the kidneys often develop as a complication of diseases elsewhere in the body, such as *diabetes mellitus, sickle-cell anemia,* and *multiple myeloma.* Kidney func-

See also
Cancers
Diabetes mellitus, type I ("juvenile")
Diabetes mellitus, type II ("adult-onset")
Excretory system
Hypertension
Inflammation
Kidney and bladder stones
Kidneys
Multiple myeloma
Polycystic kidney disease
Sickle-cell anemia
Wilms' tumor

tion may also be impaired or lost because of physical injury, as in a car accident or from a hard blow to the back.

Kidneys are particularly vulnerable to injury from poisons because a large amount of blood constantly flows through the kidneys. Serious kidney damage can result from overexposure to or abuse of household cleaning solvents, fuels, and lead and other heavy metals, as well as long-term abuse of certain pain relievers (those containing phenacetin, including acetaminophen, best known as Tylenol) and anti-inflammatory medications such as hydrocortisone. At times, though, physicians may be unable to identify any apparent cause for kidney problems.

Symptoms you are likely to notice: Among the most common signs of kidney problems are pain on one side of the body just below the ribs. Depending on the disease, there may also be blood in the urine and high blood pressure (*hypertension*). Fever, swelling and fluid retention, and weight gain are among other symptoms that may be present.

Symptoms your physician may observe: If your doctor suspects a kidney disorder, an analysis of your urine will be among the first tests to be ordered. Urinalysis can help your physician identify whether you have a bacterial infection, kidney inflammation, or one of the other kidney disorders. Other diagnostic tests could include blood tests, a kidney biopsy, an ultrasound or CT scan, or a series of special kidney X rays.

Treatment options: Whenever a kidney disorder cannot be completely cured, treatment aims at maintaining as much kidney function as possible and alleviating as many of the symp-

Lifesaving kidney dialysis

About 100,000 people in the United States whose kidneys have stopped functioning depend on kidney dialysis to stay alive. They have permanently lost kidney function and are not healthy enough to undergo a kidney transplant.

The most common type of dialysis is hemodialysis, in which a machine filters the patient's blood to remove wastes and excess fluid. Tubes from a vein in the patient's arm allow the blood to flow to the dialysis machine and back. Most people must undergo 8 to 12 hours of hemodialysis a week spread out over several sessions. The treatments are usually given at an outpatient dialysis center.

Another type of dialysis, continuous ambulatory peritoneal dialysis, can be performed at home. A tube implanted in the patient's abdomen allows a special dialysis solution to flow into the abdominal cavity. The cavity is lined with tiny blood vessels, and the dialysis solution absorbs waste products and excess water from them. The dialysis fluid is then drained from the abdominal cavity. The process is repeated four to five times daily.

toms as possible. Medication and changes in fluid intake and diet are among the basics for successful treatment.

With more severe disorders the patient's kidneys may fail completely. At one time kidney failure resulted in death, but patients today have two options—kidney dialysis (see Lifesaving kidney dialysis on page 34) or a kidney transplant.

Stages and progress: Chronic kidney diseases and serious cases of some other kidney disorders can lead to kidney failure, in which the kidneys are no longer able to remove wastes from the blood. This life-threatening condition can occur rapidly as the result of a severe infection, a sharp drop in blood pressure, or other factors; or slowly over a long period during which kidney function gradually declines.

✳ Shaped like very large lima beans, the two *kidneys* are an important part of the system for removing metabolic wastes and extra water from the body. They do this by filtering the unwanted substances from the blood and then emptying the resulting urine into the bladder. Although people normally are born with two kidneys, the body can function with only one.

Size and location: Kidneys are about four inches long and two inches wide. The two are located side by side toward the back of the torso, in the area of the lower back. Each kidney contains over a million tiny filtering systems called *nephrons.* The nephrons are made up of microscopic capillaries that carry blood to be filtered and of equally small ducts to carry off wastes and excess water.

Role: The kidneys' main job is to filter wastes and unneeded water from the blood. Along with the *bladder* and associated tubes, the kidneys are often considered the *excretory,* or *urinary,* system. The wastes removed by the kidneys are dissolved in water as *urine,* which is stored in the bladder before passing through the *urethra* to leave the body.

Kidneys are also part of the circulatory system in the sense that they remove chemical wastes from blood. They act as endocrine glands by secreting hormones that aid in regulating blood pressure and figure in the body's production of bone and new red blood cells. They also regulate the composition of blood, keeping it from becoming too acid or alkaline, and con-

Kidneys

BODY SYSTEM

TYPE: GENETIC

See also
Cancers
Diabetes mellitus, type I ("juvenile")
Diabetes mellitus, type II ("adult-onset")
Excretory system
Hypertension
Inflammation
Kidney and bladder stones
Kidney diseases
Multiple myeloma
Polycystic kidney disease
Wilms' tumor

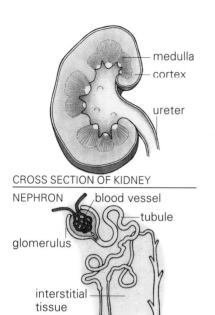

CROSS SECTION OF KIDNEY

NEPHRON

blood vessel

tubule

glomerulus

interstitial tissue

Each kidney contains about 1 million nephrons that do the actual task of filtering waste from blood. The glomeruli are knots of capillaries that bring blood to the nephron.

Kuru

DISEASE

TYPE: INFECTIOUS (BY PRION OR SLOW VIRUS)

See also
Animal diseases and humans
Creutzfeldt-Jakob disease
Guam disease
Prions and slow viruses

trol the amounts of certain substances, such as sodium and potassium.

Conditions that affect the kidneys: Kidney infections, kidney stones, inherited kidney disorders, and even cancerous tumors can interfere with the normal operation of the kidneys.

Kidney infections include *acute pyelonephritis* and *nephritis,* an inflammation of the kidney. Nephritis usually involves the small ducts in the kidney (*tubules),* the clusters of capillaries in the kidney (*glomeruli*), or the tissue between them (*interstitial tissue*).

Inherited kidney disorders include *polycystic kidney disease,* which affects kidney function, and *cystinuria,* which causes kidney stones. Inherited abnormalities also cause *reflux,* the most common urinary tract problem in children.

Kidney failure, which is the complete loss of kidney function, can be caused by infection, reaction to drugs or toxins, or even by antibodies that the immune system has produced to fight off an infectious disease. Other diseases, such as *diabetes mellitus, sickle-cell anemia,* and *multiple myeloma,* may also affect kidney function.

✳ Sometimes a disease that affects only a few people around the world has an importance that extends beyond its small number of victims because of the way that knowledge of the disease has extended medical knowledge. One such disease is the still mysterious *Guam disease.* Another is *kuru,* a disease now thought to be understood. Its principal investigator, Carleton Gajdusek, was given the 1976 Nobel Prize in Physiology or Medicine primarily because of his investigations of kuru.

In the 1950s Gajdusek, who was then studying child development in primitive cultures, learned of a previously unknown disease. Suddenly this disease had appeared among a mountain people who lived on the large island of New Guinea. Among the members of this group, known as the Fore, the disease had become the cause of half of all deaths. Gajdusek moved to the mountains of New Guinea to work with the district medical officer, Vincent Zigas, who had written the first medical reports of the disease. For seven months Gajdusek studied the disease to no avail as he lived among the Fore. He worked then and later with the United States National Institutes of Health (NIH). After Gajdusek came to work in the NIH offices in Maryland he was able to take advantage of various clues observed by pathologists and even veterinarians to unravel the mysteries of kuru.

Cause: The clues were as follows. Igor Klatzo, a neuropathologist, looked at brain samples that Gajdusek took from Fore who had died of the disease. He recognized that the samples resembled the spongy brain tissue caused by *Creutzfeldt-Jakob* (KROITS-felt YAH-kop) *disease*. In 1959 the veterinarian William Hadlow, who had read about kuru, suggested that the symptoms resemble those of *scrapie*, a disease of sheep and goats. There had been little if any connection made between scrapie and Creutzfeldt-Jakob disease at that time.

Gajdusek recognized that the clue must be in the brain. He experimented with various animals until he located those that would develop the symptoms of kuru when infected brain tissue was injected into them. This established that some infectious agent in brain tissue produced the disease.

There remained the mystery of how the disease was transmitted among the Fore. In the 1950s when the disease had become rampant, the Fore practiced ritual cannibalism, which included eating the brains of those who died. By 1985 it was generally accepted that the cause of kuru in the Fore was this practice.

Because kuru strongly resembles *mad cow disease*, which was epidemic among cattle in England in the late 1980s and early 1990s, there has been considerable concern that mad cow disease could spread by the consumption of or exposure to beef. In the mid-1990s a few cases of a disease similar to Creutzfeldt-Jakob disease did appear among the English and also the French, affecting people who probably contracted it from exposure to mad cow disease.

The actual agent of disease for kuru was termed a slow virus, primarily because there is a long incubation period—several years after exposure before the symptoms of the disease appear. Later research produced evidence that slow viruses are not viruses at all, but infectious proteins, or prions (PREE-ons).

Incidence: Kuru struck only the Fore people, a localized community in New Guinea, or other New Guineans who had married into the group and adopted its practices. It was never known to have affected Europeans or other people living among the Fore who maintained their own culture. At its height in the 1950s, it killed one out of every two members of the Fore people. Ritual cannibalism was largely abandoned in 1962 for reasons that had nothing to do with kuru, but the change resulted in kuru gradually disappearing as a disease.

Symptoms you are likely to notice: Kuru is the Fore word for "trembling," since shaking is an early symptom of the disease. The trembling is followed by dementia and death.

Symptoms a physician may observe: Examination of the brain after death reveals characteristic sponginess.

Labyrinthitis

(LAB-uhr-uhn-THYD-tuhs)

DISEASE

TYPE: INFECTIOUS
DEVELOPMENTAL

✳ A child who has a severe ear infection begins to experience dizziness and hearing loss. The suspected cause is a condition called *labyrinthitis*.

Cause: If a person has acute *otitis media* (a severe ear infection) or any form of *meningitis*, microorganisms may enter the inner ear to cause labyrinthitis. A fetus may also suffer labyrinthitis if its mother experiences "German" measles (rubella), especially during the first three months of pregnancy. When caused by exposure to the rubella virus, the condition is known as *viral endolymphatic* (EN-duh-lim-FAD-ik) *labyrinthitis*.

Symptoms you are likely to notice: The symptoms of labyrinthitis are severe vertigo or dizziness. If untreated it also results in complete hearing loss and facial paralysis.

Treatment options: A physician may suggest a procedure known as *labyrinthectomy* to drain the inner ear. Sometimes removal of mastoid glands near the ear is also recommended. In conjunction with the procedure antibiotics may be used to knock out bacteria if that is the cause of the infection.

Stages and progress: In the case of viral endolymphatic labyrinthitis the rubella virus invades the developing inner ear of a fetus and destroys much of the tissue just at the time when the cochlea and the semicircular canals are developing. The *cochlea* is the snail-shaped organ of hearing that is connected to other intricate passages to make up the inner ear. The whole complex is known as the *labyrinth* (LAB-uh-RINTH). The semicircular canals are three fluid-filled chambers in the labyrinth that give a feeling of balance.

When labyrinthitis occurs in children or adults secondary to other infections, it can damage tissue both in the cochlea, causing deafness, and in the semicircular canals, causing loss of balance and vertigo.

Prevention: To avoid the congenital deafness associated with viral endolymphatic labyrinthitis, women of childbearing age should have immunity to rubella. To prevent the condition in people of any age, all infections of the ear or other parts of the nervous system should be treated promptly.

See also
Balance
Deafness
Dizziness
Earache
Embryo
"German" measles (rubella)
Meningitis
Nausea
Otitis media
Paralysis
Vaccination and disease

✳ *Lactose intolerance* is the inability to digest the milk sugar found in ice cream, ordinary milk, and other dairy products. For people with this disorder, eating dairy products results in bloating, abdominal cramping, gas, and diarrhea. A surprisingly large number of people have lactose intolerance, which is a hereditary condition for the great majority.

Causes: Normally when people drink or eat anything containing cow's milk, the lining of the small intestine produces an enzyme called *lactase* (LAK-tays) to break down the milk sugar. With lactose intolerance the small intestine loses the ability to produce enough lactase. Instead intestinal bacteria wind up fermenting the undigested milk sugar, creating gas, acids, and the diarrhea associated with lactose intolerance.

While the disorder is most frequently inherited, it can be caused by other intestinal disorders, including *Crohn's disease*, *tropical sprue*, and *ulcerative colitis*.

Incidence: An estimated 50 million Americans have partial or complete lactose intolerance, including about 95% of Native Americans, 90% of Asian-Americans, 70% of African-Americans, 60% of Jewish-Americans, and 50% of Mexican-Americans. About 25% of Caucasian-Americans other than Jewish-Americans are lactose intolerant.

Lactose intolerance
(LAK-tohs)

DISEASE

TYPE: GENETIC

See also
Colitis
Crohn's disease
Diarrhea
Sprue

Symptoms you are likely to notice: Abdominal cramps, bloating, flatulence, and diarrhea are the most common symptoms. The severity of the symptoms varies widely, however, depending on how much lactase your body is able to produce and how much milk sugar you have eaten.

Symptoms your physician may observe: Lactose intolerance produces symptoms similar to those of other intestinal disorders and may be the result of one of them. Your doctor will look for other symptoms, such as weight loss, which could indicate that another disorder is involved.

Treatment options: Some people restrict or avoid eating milk products altogether. Others use nonprescription lactase replacement caplets, which are taken just before eating milk products.

Stages and progress: While most babies have high levels of lactase, the ability to produce this enzyme often declines during adolescence and adulthood, especially for people who are not of European ancestry. Thus lactose intolerance is normal for as much as 70% of the world's population.

Large intestine

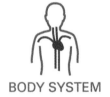

BODY SYSTEM

The main role of the large intestine is removal of fluids from food waste. Millions of helpful bacteria usually are present, breaking down and further liquefying the waste matter as it passes through.

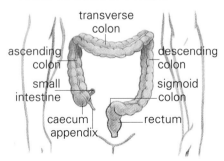

✳ The digestive tract is the part of the human body that processes food and removes its nutrients for use as energy and building blocks of the body. Most of the removal process takes place in long folded tubes called the small and the *large intestine*, collectively referred to by biologists as the *gut*. Physicians often call the intestines the *bowels*.

After most of the nutrients in food are gone, the remains of food move out of the small intestine and pass into the five-foot-long large intestine as a kind of soup. Water is extracted from the soup through the walls of the large intestine. Most of the large intestine is the section called the *colon* (KOH-luhn), which is between the opening of the small intestine and the rectum.

Size and location: The small intestine connects to the large on the lower right side of the body at the bottom of the abdomen. The connection is not at the end, but a few inches away from the end of the large intestine. The dead end section below the connection is called the *caecum* (SEE-cum). The *appendix* is attached to the bottom of the caecum.

The main part of large intestine has nowhere to go but up, and so it does for a while. This part is called the *ascending colon*. When the ascending colon reaches the vicinity of the *liver*, which is a large organ occupying much of the lower abdomen, the intestine turns sharply to the left and becomes horizontal as it crosses the abdominal cavity. This section is known as the *transverse colon*; it passes under the liver, stomach, and pancreas. When it reaches the other side of the cavity, it turns down again to form the *descending colon*. There is then an S-shaped section called the *sigmoid colon* that enables the end of the large intestine to be centered in the body at the back. A short straight stretch leading to the anal opening for waste discharge is called the *rectum*. Sometimes the rectum is counted as part of the large intestine, but often it is treated as a separate organ.

All in all, from caecum to rectum, the typical large intestine is about five feet long.

Role: Virtually the only role of the large intestine is to remove water from food residues and transport that water into the bloodstream. The water is accompanied by minerals that dissolve in water, notably such metals as sodium and potassium, as well as chlorine. Without these minerals, known collectively as *electrolytes,* the blood is chemically unbalanced, a condition that can be fatal.

A large colony of various bacteria that inhabit the large intestine further digest food, releasing in the process some of the mineral compounds that dissolve in the water that is transported into the blood. These bacteria also produce gases that form bubbles in the fecal matter; the gas is discharged through the anus.

Conditions that affect large intestine: While the normal colony of bacteria in the large intestine contributes to absorption of nutrients from food, it frequently happens that certain species or strains of bacteria produce toxins that damage the walls of the intestine. The body reacts in several ways. Food wastes may be processed too quickly in an effort to rid the body of the irritating bacteria. When this happens, water is not removed because of the short time the wastes spend in the intestine. Feces produced are thin and watery, a condition known as *diarrhea.* Diarrhea also results if the inflammation of the walls

See also
Abscess
Appendicitis
Autoimmune diseases
Bacteria and disease
Cancers
Colitis
Congenital digestive system conditions
Constipation
Crohn's disease
Cryptosporidiosis
Diarrhea
Digestive system
Diverticular diseases
***E. coli* infection**
Food poisoning
Gastroenteritis
Giardia
Hemorrhoids
Hernias
Ileus
Inflammation
Irritable bowel syndrome
Parasites and disease
Pinworms
Rectum
Sprue
Tapeworm
Viruses and disease
Whipworm

of the intestine produces swelling that effectively seals the walls, keeping the fluids from passing through. Although bacteria are the source of toxic attacks on intestinal walls, viruses can also interfere with operation of the intestines by causing tissues to be inflamed and to swell up. In this case, the immune system is probably the actual cause of the symptoms as it tries to rid the body of the viral infection.

Certain parasites, notably amoebas, also produce toxins or otherwise halt the operations of the large intestine. A common problem is *giardia*, in which a parasite attaches itself to the intestinal wall. Some parasites can live in the large intestine for long periods of time without producing acute symptoms but generally debilitating the body. Among these are tapeworms, pinworms, and whipworms.

The large intestine is also subject to a number of chronic conditions that are genetic or of unknown origin. The genetic factor that makes some people more likely to develop *colon cancer* is now known. Often such a cancer is preceded by small projections of the intestinal lining called *polyps*. Somewhat similar in nature to polyps but pointed the other way are the pockets known as diverticuli; these are subject to the inflammation called *diverticulitis*. *Crohn's disease* is thought to be an autoimmune reaction, but the causes of the somewhat similar *irritable bowel syndrome* and *ulcerative colitis* are both unknown. All three diseases produce spells of diarrhea and discomfort; in the case of Crohn's disease symptoms may be severe enough for sections of the intestine to be removed.

Laryngitis
(LAR-uhn-JY-tis)

DISEASE

TYPE: INFECTIOUS
ENVIRONMENTAL

✳ If a person with a cold spends an evening cheering on a favorite sports team, it is not surprising if he wakes up the next day having "lost his voice." The cause is *laryngitis*, an inflammation of the voice box, or larynx.

Causes: The most frequent cause of laryngitis is an upper respiratory infection such as the *common cold*. However, laryngitis can occur with more serious illnesses including *bronchitis, pneumonia, influenza, pertussis, measles,* and *diphtheria*. Sometimes the condition is brought about through environmental causes, as when the voice is used excessively or when irritating smoke or fumes are inhaled. A sudden temperature change may also bring about laryngitis.

Symptoms you are likely to notice: Laryngitis symptoms include hoarseness or total loss of voice with a tickling, raw feeling in the throat. Usually there is no pain. A mild fever may also ensue.

Symptoms your physician may observe: A physician may notice on examination that the moist mucous membranes of the throat are swollen. The movement of the vocal cords within the larynx or voice box may also be somewhat reduced.

Treatment options: If the respiratory infection is bacterial, then prescription antibiotics will help to cure the primary disorder and the hoarseness will soon disappear. Home remedies to reduce laryngitis symptoms include drinking warm liquids, resting the voice, using cough syrup, swallowing lozenges, and inhaling steam. Drinking iced beverages and alcohol should be avoided. If the air in the home is too dry, a humidifier should be used to moisten it and care should be taken to eliminate irritants such as cigarette smoke or fumes. Whispering to communicate is not recommended because this may cause as much damage to the vocal cords as yelling.

Stages and progress: If laryngitis persists for two weeks, fever is high, or an acute condition exists in children under five, medical care to discover other underlying causes is recommended. A related, more serious condition is *laryngismus* (LAR-uhn-JIZ-muhs), uncontrolled spasms of the voice box usually caused by inflammation.

Prevention: Care should be taken to treat the symptoms of respiratory infections promptly so that laryngitis does not develop. If using the voice excessively is anticipated, precautions should be taken such as lubricating the throat with lozenges. Try not to strain the vocal cords.

See also
Bronchitis
Common cold
Diphtheria
Influenza
Larynx
Measles (rubeola)
Pertussis
Pneumonia

✳ The *larynx*, or voice box, contains the two vocal cords we use to produce speech. Muscles and ligaments hold together the nine bits of cartilage that help hold the shape of the larynx. The largest cartilage section, the *thyroid cartilage*, causes the bulge at the front of the neck, called the Adam's apple.

Size and location: Just over 1° inches long, the larynx is part of the upper respiratory system. It lies just below the

Larynx
(LAR-ingks)

BODY SYSTEM

See also
Cancers
Laryngitis
Respiratory system
Trachea

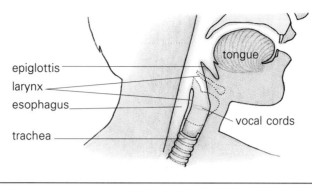

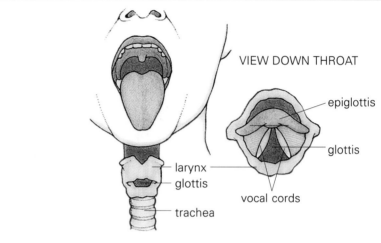

The complex bits and pieces that make up our vocal apparatus enable human speech. Our nearest relatives, the great apes, lack this complexity and cannot make speech sounds. Damage to the larynx from accident or from tumors can make ordinary speech impossible, but modern electronic aids enable people with damaged vocal cords to produce recognizable speech.

epiglottis, which is at the bottom of the throat, or *pharynx* (FAR-ingks), and which closes off the airway when you swallow foods or liquids. The bottom of the larynx is connected to the *trachea* (TRAY-kee-uh), which extends to the lungs.

Role: The larynx produces the sounds we use to speak. Air exhaled from the lungs passes through the *glottis,* the opening in the larynx, and vibrates the two elastic vocal cords located on either side of the opening. The vibration produces raw sounds that we then shape into speech with our mouths.

The larynx also closes off the airway when you swallow foods or liquids. Each time you swallow, the larynx moves upward slightly to make contact with the epiglottis, the flap of tissue just above it. This motion effectively seals off the larynx and the rest of the airway below it. When it is closed properly, foods and liquids slide safely past it and into the esophagus. Sometimes, however, when you swallow too fast, food or liquids "go down the wrong pipe" because the larynx and epiglottis have not sealed completely.

Conditions that affect the larynx: Probably the most common condition associated with the larynx is *laryngitis,* an inflammation that causes hoarseness or complete loss of voice for a time. Tumors, both cancerous and noncancerous, can grow in the larynx. Paralysis of one or both vocal cords sometimes results from tumors and other disorders.

✳ Perhaps the earliest environmental pollution caused by humans was metallic lead. Archaeological evidence for smelted lead exists from 6000 B.C. It is not known when people first recognized that lead is dangerous, although warnings against *lead poisoning* exist among early Greek medical writings.

Cause: Lead poisoning occurs when many lead compounds are eaten or drunk, applied to the skin, or breathed. Metallic lead is not poisonous to the touch but it is dangerous when eaten or breathed. Acute lead poisoning was first noticed among miners and people who processed lead ores, but today the main concern comes from exposure to low levels of lead, which lowers measurable intelligence in children.

Lead compounds have many virtues and, despite the danger, are still in use. Among the sources of lead in the environment that are of current concern are the following:

Old paint: Although modern paints for use in places that might cause lead poisoning are manufactured without lead, paint that contains high levels of lead coats interior as well as exterior walls in older buildings throughout the industrialized world. The main danger is that old paint often falls off walls in small pieces. Children find that these paint flakes are somewhat sweet and eat the chips, causing lead poisoning.

Dishes: Although dishes have come a long way from the lead jars of the Romans and the lead-alloyed pewter plates of the American colonists, some forms of ceramics continue to use lead glazes and decorative paints or dyes based on lead. The ceramics in question are primarily the shiny forms, called porcelains or enamels. The less shiny stoneware, unless painted or decorated, has negligible levels of lead. Ceramic tableware is considered the largest source of dietary lead today.

Plumbing: Environmentalists have measured household water for lead leaching from faucets. In some samples of a pint of water drawn through a faucet, lead reached levels as high as

Lead poisoning

INJURY

TYPE: ENVIRONMENTAL

See also
Colic
Diet and disease
Environment and disease
Poisoning

25 times the allowable maximum daily intake. The laboratory that did the testing estimated that about 25% of faucets used in the United States leach dangerous levels of lead. Such leaching may diminish as faucets age.

Calcium supplements: Lead often travels with calcium. Calcium supplements are offered as pills or added to some products, especially drinks likely to be consumed by children. Antacid tablets are also often promoted as calcium supplements. Some of the sources of calcium are safe chemicals concocted in laboratories, but ground bone and lead-laced calcium-rich earths (dolomite) or minerals (calcium carbonate, also known as limestone) are also used. A study of calcium supplements showed that more than 50 of them also contained lead, 17 in amounts higher than the 6 micrograms a day that is the maximum allowable limit for children under six years old. Bonemeal-based supplements were the worst offenders, but it is not clear that the lead is actually from the bonemeal.

Occupational exposure: Adults exposed to lead at work often develop lead poisoning. It was from work-related lead poisoning that the symptoms of lead poisoning, which can affect not only the nerves, but also the stomach, testes, kidney, and bone marrow, were first noticed. Inhaled lead dust can also adversely affect the lungs. Among the occupations hazardous for lead today are those involved with storage batteries, pottery manufacture, plumbing and heating, machine maintenance and repair, home renovation, and ship or office construction.

The danger of environmental lead, recognized for centuries, has not disappeared. Old paint containing lead is the most hazardous, mainly to children; but the cumulative effect of lead from plumbing, some ceramics, calcium supplements, or other sources can cause subtle damage to the nervous system.

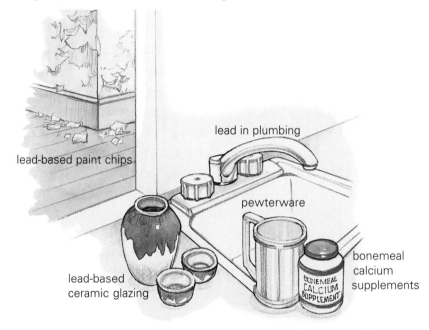

lead-based paint chips

lead in plumbing

pewterware

lead-based ceramic glazing

bonemeal calcium supplements

BONEMEAL CALCIUM SUPPLEMENT

Incidence: Fatal lead poisoning is no longer common, but the U.S. Centers for Disease Control and Prevention (CDC) has declared lead poisoning to be the most common preventable childhood disease. The main concern is lowered intelligence, but there may be other harmful effects of low-level lead poisoning. The CDC estimates, in the absence of national tests, that 4 to 6 million American children exceed its standard of 10 micrograms per deciliter.

Symptoms you are likely to notice: Lead poisoning may be *acute* from the exposure to a large amount of lead over a short period of time. More often, however, it is *chronic* as a result of many small exposures over a long period of time. Because lead is chemically similar to calcium, the body tends to retain it with the same mechanisms used for holding on to calcium. The difference, of course, is that calcium is necessary for life, but lead poisons—in part by replacing calcium and inactivating vital processes.

• *Acute lead poisoning:* The mouth and esophagus may react to the passage of a lead compound with a strong burning sensation. There will be stomach pain and intestinal distress, which may take the form of either diarrhea or constipation. As the lead gets into the nervous system, it will produce dementia and eventually paralysis of the arms or legs or both followed by seizures and complete collapse. Death can easily result.

• *Chronic lead poisoning:* In the beginning there are no symptoms. As lead builds up in the body, it may provoke irritability and loss of appetite. There may be even more subtle changes, such as lowered intelligence. Slightly higher exposure produces some of the symptoms of acute lead poisoning.

Symptoms your physician may observe: Anemia may be present early. Specific tests can now reveal even small amounts of lead in blood. Before 1991 the CDC had said there was no cause for alarm until lead levels in blood reached 25 micrograms per deciliter. Since a reevaluation in 1991, levels higher than 10 micrograms per deciliter have been considered dangerous by the CDC.

Treatment options: In the case of acute lead poisoning from eating or drinking a lead compound, the stomach is cleaned out by using magnesium sulfate or sodium sulfate.

In 1993 a study demonstrated that aggressive treatment of lead poisoning in children results in increased scores on IQ tests at a rate of about one point for each 3 micrograms per deciliter of lead reduction. The most successful treatments reduced lead levels in children with high exposures by 30 micrograms per deciliter.

Stages and progress: High levels of lead cause symptoms of poisoning, but it has long been argued that even low levels of lead in children reduce intelligence. Later in life lead may cause similar damage in adults, usually pregnant or lactating mothers and older adults with osteoporosis. Because lead travels with calcium, 90% of retained lead accumulates in the bones of the body. In pregnancy, lactation, or osteoporosis, the harmless calcium is leached from the bones, but at the same time the tagalong and very dangerous lead moves into the blood. From there it can affect various organs, impairing the mind and the operation of the body. Also, the milk of lactating mothers, who are taking calcium from the bones for milk creation, can contain lead in amounts harmful to the nursing baby.

Prevention and risk factors: In most cities, lead from faucets and pipes can be minimized by letting water run for a few seconds before using it. However, if lead is leaching from pipes it make take a minute or two to discharge all the lead-tainted water if the water system has not been used for several hours. When lead pipes are used to connect a house to the mains, as in Chicago, running water for a short time does not help.

If a calcium source is lead free, taking extra calcium along with food lowers rates of lead absorption by the body.

History: About 400 B.C. Hippocrates of Cos was among the first to document illness caused by lead mining. The modern history of lead poisoning is usually dated to 1723, when drinkers from North Carolina complained that rum from Massachusetts caused them to develop stomach problems and partial paralysis. Boston physicians attributed the problem to lead parts used in constructing the stills that produced the rum.

Around the end of the nineteenth century physicians in Australia discovered that children there were being poisoned by eating paint flakes or powder from painted walls. A few decades later physicians in the United States also learned that children develop lead poisoning by eating paint flakes that have peeled off of interior walls, especially in poorer neighborhoods, where paint is more likely to be allowed to peel. But it was not until 1955 that paints manufactured in the United States began to be limited in lead. In 1971 the U.S. Lead Paint Poisoning Prevention Act required that interior paint applied before 1955 must be stripped from buildings, but enforcement has been slow. The U.S. government finally banned lead in paints completely in 1980. Deaths of children from lead poisoning, always rare, continued to decline, although one child died from ingesting lead paint as recently as 1990.

Old paint was not the only cause for concern, however. Leaded gasoline was introduced for the first time commercially in 1923 and continued to be in use until the mid-1990s.

Effects on world population and health: Lead poisoning has been claimed as the cause of major societal trends. Among the best known of these claims is the idea that lead poisoning caused the decline and fall of the Roman Empire. There are various versions of this idea. One is that rich Romans were exposed to lead from plumbing and lead-lined drinking cups, causing the leaders of society to degenerate into madness. Another version has lead used as a sweetener in cheap wine, thereby affecting a broader swath of the Roman population.

A more modern version of this notion is that lower classes in modern industrial societies are less intelligent than upper classes. The reason given is that poor people live in old houses with old paint and in high-traffic neighborhoods with fumes from leaded gasoline.

Such theories are so broad that it is difficult to determine whether they are true. Most experts today think it too simplistic to attribute societal changes to lead alone, although they leave the door open for the possibility that lead has been one factor in such changes.

Leg cramps

SYMPTOM

✳ Two entirely different situations may lead to pains in the muscles of the calf, or lower leg, called *leg cramps*.

Nighttime cramps in your leg or foot, called *recumbency cramps,* can wake you unexpectedly from a deep sleep. These cramps can be painful but usually are harmless, and for most people they do not happen very often. Not exercising enough, or abruptly increasing the amount of exercise, may help cause nighttime leg cramps.

Leg cramps that occur after walking are termed *intermittent claudication* (CLAWD-ih-KAY-shun). They typically start after walking for a moderate distance at an ordinary pace or after a short distance when walking quickly. Standing still for a few moments causes these cramps to diminish, but they begin again after a similar amount of walking.

Parts affected: Any of the muscles in your thigh, calf, or foot may become cramped during the night. Claudication normally affects the calf muscles only.

Related symptoms: Cramps usually are accompanied by a sharp or aching pain and a slight bulging of the affected muscle. Trying to move the cramped muscle only makes it contract more tightly.

Associations: Leg cramps at night can result from strenuous exercise earlier in the day, or there may be no apparent single cause. Some disorders can bring on nighttime leg cramps, however, including *Parkinson's disease, diabetes mellitus, spinal cord lesions,* and *hypocalcemia,* a disease associated with calcium deficiency. Patients receiving dialysis for kidney disorders and some types of chemotherapy for cancers also may suffer leg and foot cramping at night.

Intermittent claudication is caused by *hardening of the arteries* or by *atherosclerosis.* The arteries in the legs are unable to supply the leg muscles with enough oxygen while walking. When the muscles are rested for a few moments, the oxygen deficit is made up.

Prevention and possible actions: Before exercising vigorously during the day, try stretching your muscles first. This may help prevent cramping later. Also, try exercising more frequently. Gradually increase your workout instead of trying to do too much at once. This can also help resolve intermittent claudication, permitting you to walk farther before developing leg cramps.

If you experience repeated episodes of nighttime cramping, your doctor may suggest quinine sulfate, which is available over the counter. Usually quinine is taken orally in the evening before going to bed over a period of one or two weeks. Some recent studies have raised concerns about the safety of quinine sulfate, however, so it should be taken only on a physician's advice.

Relief of symptoms: Massaging the affected muscle may relieve the pain and help relax your leg or foot muscle more quickly. Gently stretching the muscle while massaging it also helps. Nighttime cramps usually last only a few minutes and often go away by themselves.

Intermittent claudication is a sign of artery disease and should be reported to a physician. Some medications may resolve the problem and may also help prevent *heart attack, stroke,* or *heart failure* that could result from arterial disease.

✳ A serious illness that leads to pneumonia and other complications, *Legionnaires' disease*, sometimes called *legionellosis*, was discovered just 20 years ago. Medical researchers had overlooked the disease in the past because the bacteria were hard to detect by usual means. But an outbreak of pneumonia at a 1976 American Legion convention in Philadelphia finally tipped off researchers that a previously unrecognized disease was responsible. The Legionnaires' convention also gave the disease its name.

Cause: A rod-shaped bacteria called *Legionella pneumophila* causes Legionnaires' disease. The organisms are frequently found in fresh water, but until the 1976 outbreak had been overlooked by researchers. One reason is that the bacteria live inside other cells, including human cells and tiny single-celled organisms such as amoeba and protozoa. As a result they have been difficult to grow in the laboratory by the usual means, simply growing bacteria on an open food source.

Once the public health service identified the bacterium, researchers discovered that the organisms thrive in the cooling water of large air-conditioning units. The fine spray that air conditioners normally give off during operation carries the bacteria into the air. People downwind of the unit can then be infected by inhaling the bacteria. Another reason that the disease had not been discovered earlier is that large-scale air-conditioning was a relatively recent phenomenon in 1976.

Though a contaminated air-conditioning unit was the source of the famous 1976 outbreak, researchers have since discovered that is not the only way the disease can spread.

Legionnaires' disease
(LEE-juh-nairz)

DISEASE

TYPE: INFECTIOUS (BACTERIAL)

See also
Bacteria and disease
Lungs
Pneumonia
Respiratory system

Legionella can contaminate the hot-water side of tap water systems in homes and offices. In addition, dust from construction sites sometimes spreads the bacteria. However, the disease does not seem to spread directly from one person to another.

Incidence: Like the bacterium itself, Legionnaires' disease can be found in most parts of the world. Though it can strike at any time of the year, the disease is most common from June through October.

Many cases have been diagnosed in the United Kingdom and other European countries. The United States has between 25,000 and 50,000 cases a year, about 1-2% of all pneumonia cases reported.

Men are two to four times as likely to get the disease as women, and the likelihood of contracting Legionnaires' disease increases with age. Children are rarely afflicted. Middle-aged men who are cigarette smokers and people who have lowered resistance are the most likely to get Legionnaires' disease.

For some reason overnight travel sometimes leads to sporadic cases of the disease. But there is little mystery about the noticeably higher number of cases among power company employees who work near plant cooling towers, since the towers provide a perfect breeding ground for the bacteria.

Symptoms you are likely to notice: Early signs of the disease include a slight headache, a feeling of being out of sorts, fever, and chills. Other symptoms are a dry cough that steadily gets worse, chest pain, shortness of breath, and muscular pain. Nausea, vomiting, diarrhea, and abdominal pain also sometimes accompany Legionnaires' disease. *The disease is potentially very serious, and you should get prompt medical attention.*

Symptoms your physician may observe: Distinguishing Legionnaires' disease from other forms of pneumonia can be difficult when based on the outward symptoms alone. But your doctor may suspect Legionnaires' disease if you develop pneumonialike symptoms during the summer months. To be certain, a physician will have chest X rays taken and will send samples of your blood and mucus for lab tests.

Treatment options: People with Legionnaires' disease do not respond to the usual therapy for viral or bacterial pneumonia. But various antibiotics, especially erythromycin or rifampin and erythromycin together, have been found to be effective in fighting the disease.

All forms of pneumonia are serious medical conditions, however, and in severe cases of Legionnaires' disease a physician may decide hospitalization is best. If fever is high, the patient may be given fluids intravenously to replace what the body is losing. An oxygen mask may be necessary if the patient experiences trouble breathing.

Without proper treatment Legionnaires' disease is fatal in 15 to 20% of cases. The fatality rate can be as high as 50% in patients whose resistance has been already weakened by medications or ill health.

Stages and progress: Onset of Legionnaires' can begin anywhere from two to ten days after being exposed to the bacteria. But the disease has a low infection rate. Only about 5% of those coming in contact with the bacteria actually become ill.

A day or less after the first symptoms appear, your temperature will rise rapidly and you will probably experience severe chills. In about half the cases the fever reaches 104°F. You will have a steadily worsening cough that will bring up mucus (and sometimes blood). As the pneumonia worsens, you will also suffer shortness of breath and chest pains, caused by *pleurisy*. Other flulike symptoms include muscle pains, headache, and perhaps diarrhea.

The disease usually worsens for about four to six days and then levels off for four or five days. Recovery then begins, though in milder cases it may start sooner.

Most people recover completely, but a severe bout with Legionnaires' disease can have serious medical complications, including kidney failure and permanent lung and liver damage. About 15% of cases prove fatal from respiratory failure.

Prevention: Large air-conditioning units and power station cooling towers are major sources of airborne *Legionella* bacteria. Regular cleaning of these units and use of chemical additives limit or prevent growth of the *Legionella* bacteria. Keeping hot water in institutional plumbing systems at 140°F sharply reduces concentrations of the bacteria. Contaminated drinking water may be rechlorinated. Replacing washers in plumbing fittings may also help because certain types of rubber in the washers actually help promote growth of *Legionella*.

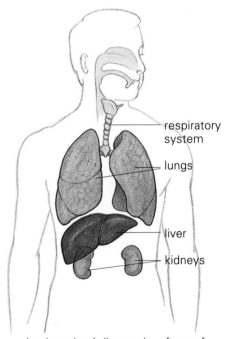

Legionnaires' disease is a form of pneumonia that may also attack other parts of the chest cavity. Infection sometimes can spread into the abdominal region. Before the advent of air conditioning and humidifiers, Legionnaires' disease was undetected. There may have been occasional instances, but the first known large-scale outbreak occurred in 1976.

Leprosy

DISEASE

TYPE: INFECTIOUS (BACTERIAL)

See also
Bacteria and disease
Tuberculosis

※ *Leprosy,* also called *Hansen's disease,* is an infectious disease that affects skin, nerves, and mucous membranes. Though slow-growing, it is one of the world's most crippling diseases.

People with leprosy have often been treated as social outcasts. In ancient times people recognized that some diseases might be contagious. Some contagious diseases with easily seen symptoms came to be called leprosy, although modern writers think that the diseases called leprosy in the past were not the same as the one now known as Hansen's disease. In the ancient Middle East people with disfiguring diseases came to be known as *lepers* and were kept out of ordinary society; they mainly lived as wandering beggars. Scientists who have studied the bones of those people have found that characteristics of Hansen's disease were absent.

Even in modern times people with Hansen's disease have been segregated from the rest of society and made to live in *leper colonies.* Because of the historical confusion between leprosy and other diseases, the modern disease is often called by its other name, Hansen's disease.

Many people with leprosy do not seek treatment because of this history. Hansen's disease, which is not easily transmitted, is popularly thought to be more infectious than it is. Because treatment still takes place in separate facilities, people with leprosy fear that they will not be allowed back into the community even after they are cured.

Cause: Leprosy is caused by a relative of the bacterium that causes tuberculosis, the bacillus *Mycobacterium tuberculosis.* The leprosy bacillus is *Mycobacterium leprae.*

Leprosy is probably spread through sneezing and coughing. The leprosy bacilli travel through the air in droplets released when people cough or sneeze. They can survive three weeks or longer outside the human body, in dust or on clothing.

Incidence: Although infectious, leprosy is one of the least contagious of all diseases. Only a small number of people with this disease are actually contagious, and with regular medication they soon become noncontagious.

Most people quickly acquire natural immunity when exposed to leprosy and have mild symptoms (sometimes called *tuberculoid leprosy*). But about 5% of the world population cannot develop natural immunity and contract the severe form of the disease, known as *lepromatous leprosy.* By some estimates as many as one-quarter of untreated patients become disabled. Leprosy is also one of the leading causes of blindness.

About 6,000 people in the United States have leprosy, and about 200 new cases develop yearly. Most leprosy patients in the United States lead completely normal lives.

Symptoms you are likely to notice: Early signs of leprosy include discolored patches on the skin. Then comes numbness in the discolored patches of skin followed by a gradual but total loss of feeling. Sometimes people have attacks of "pins and needles." Some types of the disease produce bumps on the skin.

Symptoms your physician may observe: People who experience a loss of sensation in the hands, feet, face, and other skin areas should consult a physician. The physician will look for enlargement and tenderness of one or more nerves in the affected area. The physician will also do a skin smear to check for the presence of the leprosy bacilli.

Treatment options: Several antibiotics are effective against leprosy. In the 1980s the World Health Organization (WHO) recommended a three-drug combination as standard treatment. Known as MDT, this drug combination has cured over 10 million people to date. Many cases can be cured in six months to three years. MDT usually makes a patient noncontagious within only a few days. Surgery, amputation, transplants, or cosmetic surgery may be needed to help patients regain self-esteem. Social rehabilitation is also essential.

The center for research, training, and education on leprosy in the United States is in Carville, Louisiana. Eleven other regional centers, located mostly in major cities, treat people with leprosy on an outpatient basis.

Stages and progress: When leprosy attacks the skin, it destroys nerve endings, sweat glands, hair follicles, and pigment-producing cells. It also attacks peripheral nerves, so the ability to feel light touches and hot or cold goes first. After a time the affected part may lose the ability to feel anything. Injuries, cuts, and burns that patients do not feel become a constant danger. For people who develop some immunity to leprosy, this is about as far as the disease progresses.

In those with lepromatous leprosy, the disease can wreak great devastation.

- *Nose:* If left untreated, bacilli entering the mucus lining of the nose can lead to internal damage, which in time causes the nose to collapse.
- *Eyes:* If the facial nerve is affected, one loses the blinking reflex of the eye, which can lead to blindness.
- *Hands:* If the nerve above the elbow is affected, part of the hand becomes numb and the small muscles become paralyzed. This may lead to curling or "clawing" of the fingers. Hand surgery and physical therapy can keep fingers flexible.
- *Legs:* If the nerves of the legs are affected, injury and infection can follow. Over time people with advanced leprosy may need artificial feet or legs, or wheelchairs.

Death from leprosy itself is rare, although the body is weakened and more susceptible to other diseases.

Prevention and risk factors: Researchers in the past had been unable to create a vaccine against leprosy because they were unable to grow a culture in a test tube. More recently it was learned that armadillos can develop leprosy. This provided an experimental animal for the first time, and a vaccine is now available.

History: Leprosy became epidemic in the Middle Ages in Europe. Yet it was not until 1873 that leprosy could be shown to be infectious rather than hereditary. Armauer Hansen of Norway discovered the rod-shaped leprosy bacilli.

Attitudes and traditions about leprosy in the ancient world continue to influence the way we think about the disease today. For thousands of years people with leprosy were taken to a priest for exorcism instead of to a doctor for treatment. In the Middle Ages people with leprosy were required to wear clappers or bells or to cry out "unclean" when approaching others. People with leprosy and their uninfected children were banished from their communities and confined in leper colonies.

Effects on world population and health: Leprosy, although uncommon in the United States, continues to be a major international health problem. This is especially true in developing countries where conditions of poverty, poor health, and poor hygiene are common. India has the most cases, followed by Brazil and Myanmar.

✳ *Leukemia* is a general term for various life-threatening cancers that affect bone marrow, the lymphatic system, or other tissues involved in forming blood cells. White blood cells, also called *leukocytes*, are the essential warriors in the fight against infections and cancers. But as leukemia develops, it stimulates production of abnormal white blood cells in ever-increasing concentrations.

Eventually the abnormal cells interfere with production of other blood components, including red blood cells that carry oxygen throughout the body and platelets that help in blood clotting. Shortages of these important blood cells affect the functioning of vital organs by cutting off the supply of oxygen to the cells that make them up. The body also has greater and greater trouble in fighting off infections because as the cancer spreads there are fewer healthy white blood cells to fight bacteria and other invading organisms.

Leukemias are classified according to how quickly they progress and which type of white blood cell they affect, such as the *lymphocytes* or one of the *phagocytes*. (See Lymphocytes; Phagocytes and other leukocytes.) A chronic leukemia develops comparatively slowly and symptoms may not appear for some time. An acute leukemia progresses quickly and is characterized by a rapid increase in immature white blood cells.

Basic types of leukemia include the following:

• *Acute lymphocytic leukemia* (ALL) usually affects children and so is sometimes called childhood leukemia. The disease can appear suddenly and cause the body to overproduce immature lymphocytes; such immature white blood cells are called *blasts*.

• *Chronic lymphocytic leukemia* (CLL) usually strikes people over 50 years of age. This cancer causes overproduction of mature lymphocytes.

• *Acute nonlymphocytic leukemia* (ANLL) is the most common form of leukemia in adults. It can develop quickly and cause the bone marrow to overproduce immature granulocytes, which like other immature white blood cells are called blasts.

• *Chronic myelogenous leukemia* (CML) affects the white blood cells called granulocytes, causing the bone marrow to overproduce abnormal cancerous versions of them. The disease progresses slowly and often strikes people in middle age.

Leukemia
(loo-KEE-me-uh)

DISEASE

TYPE: CANCER

See also
Cancers
Environment and disease
Immune system
Lymphocytes
Phagocytes and other leukocytes
Viruses and disease

Causes: Medical researchers do not know precisely what causes leukemia, but some believe that susceptibility to it can be inherited. The disease has been found to occur at a higher rate in some families. Other possible causes or contributing factors may include viruses and chemicals. Exposure to repeated small doses of radiation or to a single large dose may also cause leukemia.

Incidence: Leukemia is a relatively rare form of cancer, accounting for only about 5% of all cancers worldwide. For every 100,000 people only about 10 contract leukemia. About 85% of all childhood leukemias are ALL, although adults also suffer this disease and in greater overall numbers. CLL almost always strikes people over 40 years of age and is about twice as likely to occur in men as women.

Symptoms you are likely to notice: Acute forms of leukemia often (but not always) develop symptoms fairly suddenly. Though they may vary according to type, symptoms can include fatigue, headaches, fever, pain in the bones and joints, bruising, bleeding from the gums or mucous membranes, and swollen lymph nodes. Chronic leukemias, which progress slowly, may not produce any noticeable symptoms.

Symptoms your physician may observe: All leukemias eventually result in anemia, fatigue, a tendency to bleed, and an increased susceptibility to infection. They may cause swelling of the lymph nodes, spleen, or liver.

Blood tests and biopsy of the bone marrow—examination of a sample of bone marrow under a microscope—are the surest ways to diagnose leukemia and to determine which type you have contracted.

Treatment options: Chemotherapy, often in combination with radiation and bone marrow transplants, has been used with varying degrees of success in treating the various types of leukemia. Bone marrow transplants make higher doses possible in chemotherapy programs and provide a source of noncancerous cells that produce normal leukocytes.

Other forms of treatment are being researched, including the transplant of umbilical cord blood collected during normal births. This blood contains the critical stem cells that are progenitors of all blood cells.

Stages and progress: Whether the leukemia progresses slowly or quickly, it is fatal without successful medical treatment. Treatment, however, often arrests or eliminates the disease.

• *ALL:* Onset of this leukemia may be sudden, and it may take only days or weeks for symptoms to develop. Without treatment, bleeding and infection lead to death within months. Younger children who contract this disease have a better chance of being cured than older children and adults.

• *CLL:* Development of CLL can be gradual, and it is usually discovered through routine blood tests. Since CLL causes overproduction of functioning mature white blood cells, some patients can survive for years even without medical treatment. At times this leukemia progresses more rapidly, however.

• *ANLL:* This leukemia progresses very rapidly and can cause death in a matter of weeks if not treated successfully. It is also more difficult to cure. Of patients who enter remission as a result of chemotherapy, about 80% suffer relapses. Patients with this form of leukemia often have certain characteristic abnormalities of their chromosomes.

• *CML:* Because this leukemia develops so slowly, it is often discovered accidentally during routine blood tests. About 90% of all people with CML have an abnormal chromosome, called the Philadelphia chromosome. The disease usually reaches an acute phase in about five years. At this time overabundance of immature white blood cells reaches a peak, and lack of blood platelets leads to serious problems with bleeding. Treating the acute phase is especially difficult; and without an intensive program of high-dose chemotherapy, radiation, and bone marrow transplants, death will follow.

Lice

DISEASE

TYPE: PARASITIC

❋ They are called cooties or crabs and are so small that it is hard to see them without a magnifying glass. They can live on any part of the body that has hair, where they cement clusters of eggs to the hair shafts. They crawl from place to place, puncturing the skin and sucking blood. They are *lice.*

Cause: Three species of lice affect humans. *Pediculosis capitis,* or head lice, infest the scalp. *Pediculosis corporis,* body lice, inhabit clothing and bedding and bite the skin they contact. *Pediculosis pubis,* pubic lice, are found in the pubic hair around the genitals.

See also
Parasites and disease
Typhus

Lice are often called crabs because they look like tiny crabs. They are a bit more than 1/16 inch long, the size of a sesame seed. Their tiny, white, elongated eggs are called nits; the eggs hatch into larvas. All three generations can be found on the body at the same time.

Lice feed on human blood and move from place to place by crawling. They attach to the skin of the human host and bite to suck out the blood.

Incidence: Outbreaks of head lice occur frequently among young children in day-care centers, elementary schools, and day camps. These outbreaks can occur at any time, but are seen most often in September. Body lice often are associated with lack of cleanliness; they tend to be found in clothing that is not cleaned regularly. Pubic lice are usually passed from one person to another during intimate sexual contact.

Symptoms you are likely to notice: Intense itching in the area of infestation is usually the first sign that a person has lice. The person may also notice the lice themselves or clusters of nits attached to body hairs. (A handheld magnifying glass is useful for this observation.)

Symptoms your physician may observe: The physician may diagnose lice infestation by observing lice or nits, or by observing puncture marks where the lice have fed.

Treatment options: Body and pubic lice infestations are usually treated with medicated lotions. Some of the lotions can be purchased without a prescription but others require a prescription. The lotion is put on liberally to cover the affected area and is left on overnight. It is then washed off and clean clothing is put on. Special shampoos are used to get rid of head lice; a special comb, called a nit comb, can help remove the eggs. To be sure that all stages of the louse life cycle are destroyed, the treatment is repeated after seven to ten days.

Lice and their eggs sometimes get onto the eyebrows and eyelashes. Petroleum jelly rather than medicated lotion is used to destroy lice in these sensitive areas.

All clothing, towels and bedding the infested person had contact with should be washed in hot water and dried in a dryer or dry-cleaned. All individuals in a household should be treated at the same time to prevent any further spread.

Antibiotics may be prescribed if scratching the infestation has caused an infection.

Stages and progress: It can take two to three weeks after lice inhabit the body before intense itching begins. This is the length of time it takes the eggs to hatch and grow into adults. Although body lice can carry *typhus,* a serious disease, the most common complication of untreated lice infestation is secondary infection caused by scratching too hard.

Untreated, the infestation increases and can spread to others through shared clothing, towels, bedding, and sexual contact.

Prevention: Head lice in children are very common. It is important to look for lice and nits whenever a child scratches his or her head a lot. If lice are found, notify the public health department or school so that an outbreak can be prevented.

Body lice can be prevented by good housekeeping practices. Thorough, frequent cleaning of clothing and linens reduces the likelihood of body lice infestations. Sharing only clean clothing can reduce the possibility of lice finding new hosts.

Pubic lice are more of an embarrassment than a health hazard. Prompt treatment of all sex partners will prevent the spread to others.

Effects on health: Lice can be uncomfortable and irritating, but they are not a major health hazard. Learning the symptoms assists in prompt treatment. Some individuals have so much experience with lice that they can successfully treat themselves or their children with the medicated lotions and shampoos available at the local pharmacy.

It saved more lives in World War II than any weapon

World War II, in the late 1930s and early 1940s, was the largest conflict between nations in recorded history. Battles raged in all parts of Europe, in Asia, in Africa, and across much of the Pacific Ocean. Over 400,000 Americans died in the war, most of them as a direct result of fighting. But near the end of the war a serious epidemic of typhus was killing American, European, and Asian soldiers faster than any weapons.

At the beginning of World War II the Swiss scientist Paul Müller had discovered that a chemical known as DDT is a powerful killer of insects, including lice.

By the end of the war DDT in powder form was being produced. Soldiers were dusted with DDT powder, which stopped the epidemic by killing the lice that transmitted typhus. Later scientists calculated that without DDT far more soldiers and civilians would have died from typhus than had been killed from all the weapons of war.

By the early 1960s, however, the widespread use of DDT was recognized as a possible health problem itself. DDT was banned for most uses in the 1970s in the United States.

Ligaments

BODY SYSTEM

The ribbons of ligament overlap at a joint, protecting it as well as holding the bones together.

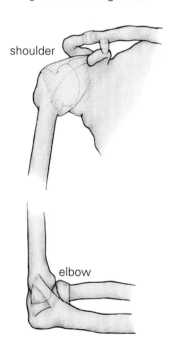

shoulder

elbow

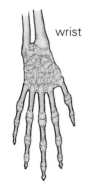

wrist

✳ Bones are attached to each other by flexible tissues called *ligaments*. A few bones, such as those in the skull, grow together, forming rigid attachments; these are not held in place by ligaments. Every place that two bones connect with each other, whether by fusing into a rigid suture or by flexible ligaments, is called a *joint*.

Size and location: Ligaments are found at all the joints where two bones are connected so that they can move, whether the movement is relatively free, as in the shoulder, or quite restricted, as in the rib joints. Although one may think of ligaments as something like rubber bands, they are more like sheets of plastic than like bands. Usually there are several overlapping ligaments at each joint, surrounding the joint on all sides.

Role: The main role of the ligaments is to connect bones at movable joints. Without ligaments, the skeleton would fall apart.

Most ligaments are made chiefly of collagen; these ligaments are white and do not stretch easily. The only ligaments that are truly elastic are the yellow ones that are found in the neck. These are yellow because they are made from the protein elastin as well as collagen. It is the elastin that enables the yellow ligaments to stretch.

Ligaments also provide the outer surfaces of the joints. Inside the ligaments there is a space that contains the smooth membrane and lubricating liquid that allows joints to move easily.

In some cases the ligaments themselves have a role beyond connection. A notable example is in the arch of the foot, which, although it contains bones, is shaped primarily by ligaments. The ligaments of the arch are the shock absorbers of the body, with a role similar to that of shock absorbers in automobiles.

Conditions that affect the ligaments: For most people the main problem that affects ligaments is overextension as a result of moving a joint in a direction it is not intended to go in or moving it farther than the nonelastic ligament allows. The damage to ligaments that occurs from this cause is called a *sprain*. A minor *strain* may involve stretched ligaments, but when the ligaments tear, healing time increases. *Tennis elbow* often consists of a minor sprain along with inflammation of the tendon where it is attached to a ligament.

Ligaments are made primarily of collagen, and for reasons that are poorly understood, collagen is sometimes attacked by the immune system. The main damage of many collagen diseases is not to the collagen of the ligaments, however, but to the collagen in skin or other organs. One of the most common of the collagen diseases, *systemic lupus erythematosus (SLE),* may attack the collagen in the joints, producing arthritis that is similar to rheumatoid arthritis. In rheumatoid arthritis itself, however, the attack of the immune system focuses on the membrane between the joints rather than on the ligaments.

See also
Autoimmune diseases
Fractures, dislocations, sprains, and strains
Hernias
Skeleton
Systemic lupus erythematosus (SLE)
Tennis elbow and related problems

※ The liver is the main chemical factory of the body and, after the skin, the largest organ in the body.

Liver

BODY SYSTEM

Size and location: The liver is a large dark red mass that can be separated into four distinct chunks, called *lobes.* Each lobe is about the same in most ways although somewhat different in size. Beyond the lobes and some fatty tissue that separates them, most of the liver appears to be an undivided mass. It weighs some three to four pounds, considerably more than the heart, stomach, or lungs, the other large organs of the abdominal cavity. In a living person the liver actually weighs more than that because it is filled with blood—at any one time from 25 to 30% of all the blood in the body is in the liver.

The liver is located near the top of the abdomen below the diaphragm. It is normally high enough to be surrounded by the lower ribs. Below the liver the stomach and intestines fill most of the remainder of the lower abdomen.

Role: If, for some reason, a person loses the liver function completely, death follows within a day. Thus the liver is a *vital organ,* one like the brain, heart, and lungs that is necessary for life. Unlike the heart or lungs, however, which have essentially only a single task each, the liver is engaged in a wide variety of functions.

As part of the digestive system, the liver acts as a ducted or exocrine gland that produces *bile,* a substance that helps reduce the acidity of the nutrient mixture and also helps break down fats with a detergent action. The liver is also part of the circulatory system, since it cleans poisons out of the blood and regu-

See also
Alcoholism
Cancers
Cirrhosis of the liver
Drug abuse
Gallstones
Hepatitis A and E
Hepatitits B and similar diseases
Jaundice
Malaria
Parasites and disease
Poisoning

lates blood's composition in various other ways. The liver also scavenges unwanted chemicals from the blood, takes them apart, and reassembles the parts into needed chemicals or into wastes.

Among the important chemicals produced by the liver are cholesterol, which, despite its unsavory reputation, is necessary for life as it is the chief component of all cell membranes; glycogen, the starchlike substance used to store sugary glucose for use when needed; urea, the form in which wastes from nitrogen compounds, such as proteins and DNA, are prepared to leave the body; and the blood proteins that are used in clotting.

Conditions that affect liver: The liver is subject to infection by bacteria and some parasites, but the most common liver infections are from several different viruses; the diseases caused by viral liver infections are all called *hepatitis,* as are other conditions, including chemical poisoning, that produce liver inflammation. Parasites include worms called *flukes* and protists called *amoebas* may also infest the liver.

Chronic inflammation of the liver leads to a condition called *cirrhosis,* in which liver cells are displaced by fat and scar tissue.

Almost any disease that seriously affects liver function can be recognized by *jaundice,* a yellowish cast to skin and eyes that is produced when the liver cannot process used red blood cells.

Although stones do not form in the liver itself, they often form from cholesterol in the gallbladder. If the stones plug the

A view of the liver

The ancients could not help but be aware of the liver, since it is the largest internal organ in humans. Livers of nonhumans were important as food items and for use in foretelling the future. Ancient writers such as Galen recognized three principal organs, the heart, the brain, and the liver—and often the liver seemed to be the most important. Indeed, a well functioning liver is essential to health. In European countries today, especially France, worrying about the state of one's liver is a national preoccupation.

The ancient Greeks developed the original form of a system of health; it was based on four fluids called *humors*: blood, phlegm, yellow bile (choler), and black bile. Whichever humor dominated determined whether a person was sanguine, phlegmatic, choleric, or bilious. Although the concept survived well into the sixteenth century, it was based on many errors. Most striking is that there is only one color of bile. Fresh bile may be somewhat more yellowish than older blacker bile, but it is the same kind of bile.

Bile is bitter. One of its other names is *gall,* a word still used for the emotional state that is also called bitter. Gall is also used as a synonym for impudent bravery. Thus it is not surprising that the liver also represented bravery in general. The alliterative expression lily-livered refers to a coward. If the liver was like a lily in any way, it could not be that of a strong-willed human.

passage of bile from the liver through the gallbladder to the stomach, the liver is affected by its own bile backing up into cells.

Chemicals of one kind or another may prove to be more powerful than the liver's ability to convert them to harmless substances. In that case the chemicals may damage the liver. This is true of various hydrocarbon vapors that are used in handling paints or in other applications. It is also true of ethyl alcohol, the active ingredient in beer, wine, and liquor. Most people do not drink enough alcohol at a single time to cause acute alcohol poisoning, but many more drink enough for long periods of time to produce cirrhosis of the liver. Nearly half of all instances of liver cirrhosis stem from alcohol abuse.

Cancers rarely begin in the liver, but liver cancer is a common form of cancer that is nearly always fatal.

Among the astonishing feats of the liver is its power to regrow from small pieces of itself. While simpler organisms can regenerate a lost tail or even, in the case of starfish, a whole body from a part, the liver and skin are the only organs in humans that can regenerate themselves. Even with this power, the liver is often defeated by its many enemies. As a result, death from liver diseases is currently eleventh in frequency among fatalities in the United States.

See **Tetanus**   **Lockjaw**

See **Back and spine problems**   **Lower back pain**

Lungs

BODY SYSTEM

✳ The main purpose of the respiratory system is to get oxygen to the blood and to remove carbon dioxide. Along the way the air is sampled for chemicals (smelled), partly cleaned, and frequently used to make sounds. *Lungs* are elastic sacs that are the most important organs of the respiratory system. When you inhale your two lungs expand to take in fresh air; when you exhale they contract to force air out. Each day you inhale and exhale the equivalent of about 5,000 gallons of air.

Size and location: Located on either side of the heart and to the sides of the chest, the lungs are enclosed in an airtight sac called the *pleural membrane.* Air enters a lung through a *bronchus* (BRONG-kuhs, plural *bronchi*—BRONG-kiy). The

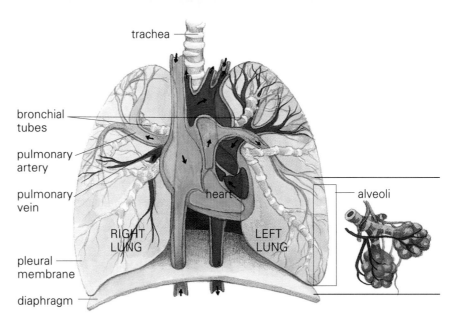

Although we think of the lungs as being essentially the same, the right lung is substantially larger than the left. This allows a space for the heart. For some illnesses the cure is a transplant of the heart and lungs together as a unit.

bronchus divides into smaller *bronchial tubes,* which continue to divide until they become very fine tubes called *bronchioles* (BRONG-kee-OLZ). Each bronchiole ends in a cluster of tiny round bodies called an *air sac.* As small as air sacs are, each of the round bodies contains even smaller cavities called *alveoli* (al-VEE-uh-LIY). It is in the thin-walled alveoli that the exchange of oxygen to and carbon dioxide from the blood actually takes place. Although each alveolus is tiny, the total surface area the alveoli is about 40 times the surface area of the skin.

The two lungs together weigh about 1.3 pounds.

Role: Lungs perform the crucial jobs of transferring oxygen from the air to the bloodstream and of filtering carbon dioxide, a waste product from the life process, out of the blood. Adults have as many as 300 million alveoli in their lungs, and the blood vessels surrounding each of these sacs absorb the oxygen. Carbon dioxide passes from the blood vessels into the alveoli so that it can be exhaled.

Conditions that affect the lungs: Because the lungs are so important, disorders that affect them can be very serious. Bacteria and viruses cause infectious diseases of the lungs, including *acute bronchitis, pneumonia, pleurisy,* and *tuberculosis.* A lung *abscess,* a pus-filled area in the lung, may be a complication of some of these diseases.

Cystic fibrosis is an inherited disease affecting the lungs. *Asthma* may be caused by allergic reactions, and breathing air filled with certain types of particles over a long period may lead to diseases like *asbestosis, silicosis,* and *emphysema.* Cigarette smoking has been linked to lung cancer and other disorders.

A stab wound that punctures a lung can cause the lung to collapse (*pneumothorax*). The lung will not expand and contract normally until the puncture has been sealed.

See **Systemic lupus erythematosus (SLE)**

Lupus erythematosus

Lyme disease

DISEASE

TYPE: TICK-BORNE (BACTERIAL)

✳ People who go into the woods or who work or play near bushes can get *Lyme disease.* With care, this serious disease can be prevented.

Cause: A bite from a deer tick can spread Lyme disease. The tick carries the disease only if the tick itself is infected with bacteria. Not everyone who is bitten by a deer tick develops the disease, but the disease is not transmitted in any other way. It cannot be caught from another person.

Incidence: Lyme disease is concentrated in suburban regions in the United States Northeast, especially Connecticut, southeastern New York State including Long Island, Massachusetts, and northern New Jersey. It is also common in the upper Midwest, especially Wisconsin and Minnesota, and on the West Coast in parts of California. Large regions, such as Wyoming, seem to be free of the disease. Outside the United States Lyme disease occurs in northern Europe.

A red region in the shape of a target or a doughnut forms around a tick bite at the start of many cases of Lyme disease. This "bull's-eye" rash is called *erythema migrans* by physicians.

Symptoms you are likely to notice: After being in the woods or even in a backyard frequented by deer, you may find a very small tick attached to your skin and feeding on blood. In the spring the tick may be as small as the period at the end of this sentence. Many people do not even notice the tick bite.

A tick bite does not mean that you will get Lyme disease, but it can alert you to other symptoms. If a characteristic *bull's-eye rash,* red with clearing at the center (see illustration) appears, go to a doctor for a test. This rash occurs in three to four out of five infections. Such a rash usually lasts for two or three weeks.

The rash does not appear in one to two out of five instances. If after being in the woods or a yard a series of flulike symp-

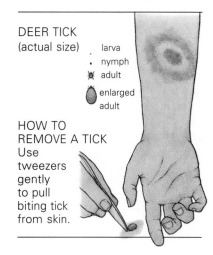

DEER TICK (actual size)
  . larva
  . nymph
  ✳ adult
  ⬮ enlarged adult

HOW TO REMOVE A TICK Use tweezers gently to pull biting tick from skin.

Parents find a new disease

In the early 1970s parents and physicians in a part of Connecticut along Long Island Sound began to notice that children from the region often developed a localized rash followed by fever, chills, and muscle aches. Some of the children also developed a form of arthritis.

One of the parents pursued the disease, and in 1975 Dr. Allen C. Steere described it to other doctors. He named it Lyme disease after the community of Old Lyme, Connecticut, where the ailment had first been noticed. Lyme disease was found to be borne by the tick *Ixodes scapularis* in 1978; the bacterium that causes the disease was identified in 1982 and later named *Borrelia burgdorferi*. Eventually researchers recognized that Lyme disease is also an illness that had puzzled doctors in Scandinavia.

toms develops, including fever, sore throat, fatigue, headache, and aching joints, see a doctor. Even if there has been no rash, you may have Lyme disease.

Symptoms your physician may observe: Lyme disease shares symptoms with many other illnesses, so one of the main tasks of the physician is to eliminate other diseases. Lyme disease is suspected primarily in regions where it is common. If other diseases are ruled out, the doctor may take a blood sample and send it to a laboratory. Results may not be available from the sample for several days. In some cases the physician may choose to begin treatment before reviewing the results of the blood test.

Treatment options: Lyme disease can be eliminated completely by the use of antibiotic drugs. Early-stage treatment may consist of pills only or a combination of shots and pills. It is important to follow the doctor's directions on how long to keep taking the medicine.

In later stages bacteria may be hidden in tissues and develop resistance. Hospitalization may be necessary in that case. Antibiotics used in hospitals for treating Lyme disease can be dangerous. Children sometimes develop gallstones from strong antibiotics; patients of any age can acquire bloodstream infections from intravenous connections.

Stages and progress: If untreated, the original flulike symptoms of Lyme disease stop after a few weeks. A new set of symptoms, often including severe headaches, emerges. Often the disease settles in the joints, producing Lyme arthritis, a painful condition that persists indefinitely without treatment. Sometimes the disease causes tics, nerve damage, or mental problems. Patients often complain of fatigue. Some report personality changes, intolerance to noise, or depression. It is not known whether the disease can damage the unborn child of a pregnant woman. Lyme disease does not lead to death.

Prevention: In regions where Lyme disease occurs, dress to keep ticks from biting in bushy or wooded areas, including backyards. Wear a long-sleeved shirt and long pants tucked into the tops of socks. A hat also helps. Ticks cannot leap or fly, so you will not be bitten unless you brush against a place where a tick is waiting. Apply an insect repellent containing the ingredient DEET or the insecticide Duranon to your clothing. *Do not use repellents or insecticides directly on your skin.* On leaving the yard or woods, shower or bathe and look carefully for ticks. Have someone remove with tweezers any tick you find. Check all over for a bull's-eye rash every time you bathe. If the rash is seen or if flulike symptoms develop after possible exposure, visit your physician at the earliest opportunity.

Discouraging deer, mice, rodents, and even (in the West) lizards from coming close to your house or commonly used yard areas can help. Keep grass mowed and avoid plants that attract deer, such as yews. Clean up brush or other places where rodents can live or obtain food. Check pets frequently for ticks.

Various insecticides will kill ticks in a limited area, such as yards or gardens. These should be applied by professionals only.

There are no vaccines available for Lyme disease, but tests are ongoing, and there is good reason to hope for success. If the vaccines work, three shots over three months will be recommended for people in areas in which Lyme disease is common.

Lymphatic system

BODY SYSTEM

✳ When blood passes through the capillaries, it loses some of its plasma, which becomes part of a liquid that is between the cells. This liquid is known as *lymph*. Lymph needs to be returned to the circulatory system to keep the blood volume fairly constant. While some liquid seeps back through capillary walls, a system of tubes called the *lymphatic system* drains some 60% of the lymph back into the blood.

Size and location: The lymphatic system is similar in many ways to the veins. Small *lymph capillaries* collect lymph. One-way valves keep it moving slowly along, although much more slowly than blood in the veins because there is no pressure similar to that caused by the pumping of the heart. The lymph vessels grow larger and culminate in two *lymphatic ducts* that drain the lymph into large veins just behind the collarbone.

Along the way lymph passes through masses of spongy tissue called *lymph nodes*; these filter out any debris, including bacteria, from the lymph. While there are lymph nodes wherever two lymph vessels are joined, they are thickest in the elbow, knee, armpit, and groin. The *spleen* is sometimes thought of as the largest of all lymph nodes, but it also has other roles.

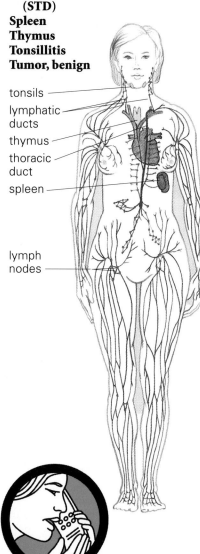

tonsils

lymphatic
ducts

thymus

thoracic
duct

spleen

lymph
nodes

The *thymus* is another specialized lymph node, but the most famous lymph nodes are the *tonsils.* Lymph nodes are sometimes called lymph glands, although they are not glands in the modern sense of the word.

Role: Lymph nodes are made from *lymphoid tissue,* but they are not the only organs where lymphoid tissue is found; it is found everywhere that bacteria or other germs can easily invade the body, specifically in the linings of the parts of the body that are exposed to the outside, such as the respiratory system and parts of the digestive system. Much of the action of the immune system takes place in lymphoid tissue. Certain white blood cells, the agranular leukocytes, form in lymph nodes, and other white blood cells are even more common in lymph than they are in blood.

Conditions that affect the lymphatic system: Whenever lymph vessels become blocked, fluids cannot drain from cells fast enough through the blood capillaries. As a result the fluids build up and produce the swelling called *edema.* Parasites that regularly block the lymph vessels can cause massive edema, known as *elephantiasis.* The much smaller swelling of *blisters* and *hives* is caused by infection, injury, or allergic reaction blocking the flow of lymph.

Cancers of the lymphatic system are relatively common. They are separated into *Hodgkin's disease* and *non-Hodgkin's lymphoma.* Hodgkin's disease is a cancer of the white blood cells called *macrophages,* while non-Hodgkin's lymphoma affects different white blood cells. Nonmalignant tumors at lymph nodes, also known as *lymphomas,* can occur as well.

Any disease that reduces the number of white blood cells or makes them abnormal and ineffective may be thought of as affecting the lymphatic system. *Leukemias* are different from lymphomas in that the site of production of the aberrant cells is the bone marrow or elsewhere instead of the lymph system. *AIDS* produces characteristic swelling of the lymph nodes along with abnormalities in white blood cells.

Infection of the lymph system, often with streptococci, causes symptoms that may be called blood poisoning, but properly are known as *lymphangitis.* Symptoms include fine red streaks radiating from a wound or bite. *This condition is a serious threat to health and needs treatment by a physician.*

✳ Although each red blood cell is almost exactly like every other, the cells we think of as white blood cells (formally known as *leukocytes)* come in at least a dozen different varieties with various roles in the immune system defense of the body. Perhaps the best known of the white blood cells are the *lymphocytes,* which form about a quarter of all the white blood cells. Another large group is the cell-devouring *phagocytes,* while the remainder include the *mast cells* and the *granulocytes,* which are largely involved in allergic reactions.

Size and location: Lymphocytes, like most cells, are microscopic. Under the microscope they can be seen to be about the same size as the red blood cells, but less regular in shape and, of course, not red. Often they are stained to make them more visible, so they may appear blue instead of white.

Although lymphocytes are known as *white blood cells,* they are found in the lymph as well as in the blood. Draining all the lymph from an animal's body will remove all the lymphocytes.

Unlike the white blood cells produced in the marrow, the lymphocytes are formed in the lymph or in the blood by cell division. As a result the daughters from one lymphocyte form a *line* of lymphocytes that are all related to each other and that share particular characteristics.

Role: The *T lymphocytes* are those that must mature in the thymus before they can be involved in the immune response. The "T" is for *thymus.* They are the principal cells involved in graft rejection, but they also have a role in fighting bacteria and other invaders, including cancer cells. The loss of one type of T cell is a major symptom of *AIDS,* although the HIV virus that causes AIDS seems to affect the immune system in many other ways as well.

The *B lymphocytes* mature outside the thymus in mammals. In birds, B lymphocytes mature in an organ that humans do not have, the bursa of Fabricius; the "B" stands for *bursa.* B cells react to invaders by releasing chemicals called *antibodies.* An antibody is a chemical that is specific to a particular protein, sugar, nucleic acid, or fat, but the strongest reaction is with proteins. If, for example, a measles virus is in the blood or lymph, a B lymphocyte will release an antibody that attaches to a protein on the surface of the virus. One kind of T cell then

Lymphocytes

BODY SYSTEM

See also
AIDS (acquired immunodeficiency syndrome)
Immune system
Lymphoma
Phagocytes and other leukocytes
SCID (severe combined immunity deficiency)
Thymus
Vaccination and disease

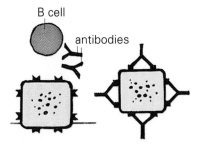

Bacteria, other cells of all kinds, and viruses expose proteins on their membranes or coats. Antibodies produced by B cells are keys that lock into specific proteins and that inactivate them. The result is that the cell or virus can no longer function.

stimulates the production of many B cells that release the same antibody. The next measles virus that comes along is met with great amounts of the antibody, causing immunity to measles.

Conditions that affect lymphocytes: Cell lines that develop cancer produce *non-Hodgkin's lymphoma.* Infection of the T cells by the HIV virus is the cause of *AIDS.*

Lymphoma

DISEASE

TYPE: CANCER

See also
Blood
Cancers
Hodgkin's disease
Immune system
Lymphatic system
Lymphocytes

✳ Cancers that develop in the lymph glands are called *lymphomas.* There are two general types: Hodgkin's disease (discussed elsewhere) and non-Hodgkin's lymphomas (discussed here).

Cause: In most cases the cause of non-Hodgkin's lymphoma is unknown. One type, Burkitt's lymphoma, which is found in Africa, is at least partly induced by exposure to the Epstein-Barr virus. The HIV virus that causes *AIDS* also appears to increase the risk of lymphoma. In some other cases suppression of the immune system plays a role; for example, people with organ transplants are at higher risk of lymphoma because of their altered immune function.

Incidence: Approximately 53,000 new cases of non-Hodgkin's lymphoma occurred annually in the United States in the late 1990s. Incidence increases with age, and the disease is more common in males than females.

Symptoms you are likely to notice: Swollen lymph glands usually are the first indication of lymphoma. Other symptoms include itching, fever, night sweats, fatigue, and weight loss.

Symptoms your physician may observe: The doctor will perform a biopsy of tissue from the lymph glands and nodes—remove tissue for examination under a microscope—to learn if cancerous cells are present and to distinguish non-Hodgkin's lymphoma from Hodgkin's disease. Other tests also may be performed, including X rays or other scans of the liver and spleen and blood chemistry analyses.

Treatment options: If the disease is localized, radiation therapy is generally the treatment of choice. In later stages of the disease both radiation and chemotherapy may be used. Some patients with advanced lymphoma may benefit from bone-marrow transplants.

Stages and progress: Initially lymphoma involves a single organ or region of lymph nodes. As the disease progresses, additional areas of the body become involved. Without treatment the disease is fatal. With early treatment about half of the patients survive at least five years following diagnosis. Even in advanced cases treatment can induce complete remission in many people.

See **Phagocytes and other leukocytes**

Macrophages

Macular degeneration

DISEASE

TYPE: MECHANICAL

See also
Detached retina
Eyes and vision
Tobacco and disease

✳ A painless disease of the eye, *macular degeneration* affects the central part of the retina, causing progressive loss of central vision. The impairment caused by macular degeneration involves a small region known as the *macula* (MAK-yool-uh) in the center of the retina. The retina is the light-sensitive nerve-filled membrane at the back of the eyeball. The macula is where the cells responsible for sharp color vision are located.

Cause: Macular degeneration typically develops when tiny amounts of blood seep through capillaries into surrounding space, causing scar tissue to form. Cells in the macula become undernourished and die. As a result the center of the retina separates from the underlying tissue of the eyeball. Sometimes the separation takes many months, but it can also happen in a matter of days. Macular degeneration differs from detached retina in that the edges of the retina stay in place.

Symptoms you are likely to notice: People with macular degeneration may first notice a tiny spot of fuzziness in the center of their vision. Normally straight lines appear wavy; colors, instead of being clear and bright, become increasingly gray. The fuzzy spot grows over time until such activities as reading at a normal distance and driving a car become extremely difficult. Eventually all that remains is peripheral vision—the ability to see out of the corners of the eye. Macular degeneration generally, but not always, affects both eyes; but it may not become apparent until the second eye begins to be damaged.

Prevention: There is no specific method for preventing macular degeneration, but the onset of the disease can be slowed by laser treatments to stop the bleeding. A daily, self-administered, at-home test is sometimes given to people who have a high probability of developing the disease. The test consists of looking at a printed grid. If the lines appear wavy or if they are indistinct in some areas, laser treatments are begun immediately. Inevitably the disease wins, and even though peripheral vision remains, the individual becomes legally blind.

A number of near-vision aids can help individuals to remain independent by maintaining the ability to navigate. These aids include high-intensity lighting and magnifying lenses.

Risk factors: Members of some families appear to be especially prone to this kind of degeneration. Macular degeneration is also associated with aging and with smoking tobacco.

Mad cow disease   *See* **Animal diseases and humans; Creutzfeldt-Jakob disease**

Malaria

DISEASE

TYPE: MOSQUITO-BORNE
        PARASITIC

See also
Anemias
Animal diseases and humans
Blood
Fever
Jaundice
Kidneys
Liver
Parasites and disease
Relapsing fevers
Sickle-cell anemia
Tropical diseases

✳ People who travel to tropical parts of the world can get *malaria*. With proper precautions this serious disease can be prevented and most cases of it cured.

Cause: A bite from a female *Anopheles* (uh-NOF-uh-leez) mosquito can spread malaria. Within the mosquito's salivary glands are the tiny microorganisms that cause the disease. These microscopic parasites belong to one of four species of *Plasmodium* (plaz-MOH-dee-uhm), a type of one-celled protist. The *Plasmodium* protists belong to a group called the sporozoans, so named because of a protective sporelike coat. When the mosquito pierces human skin to take a meal of blood, some of the organisms enter the body, travel to the liver, and then get into the bloodstream, where they reproduce asexually. Symptoms of malaria occur as the parasites undergo their reproductive cycle.

Incidence: Malaria is a tropical disease found primarily in the equatorial regions of South and Central America, Africa, and Asia. However, instances of the disease are found in North America when people who have traveled to tropical regions come home already infected with the disease. Because malaria is spread by mosquitoes, swampy regions where the insects breed are likely to be areas for malaria. Throughout the world swamps have been drained and insecticides used to destroy mosquito populations, reducing the incidence of malaria. However, mosquitoes breed in huge numbers and produce several generations in a single season. Over several decades of spraying pesticides, mosquitoes have developed resistance to pesticides that were sprayed the most. This has made eradicating the disease much more difficult.

There are 300 to 500 million people worldwide who are infected with malaria.

Symptoms you are likely to notice: The symptoms characteristic of malaria are chills, fever, shaking, profuse sweating, and fatigue. These symptoms come and go in regular waves, timed with the reproductive cycle of the parasites.

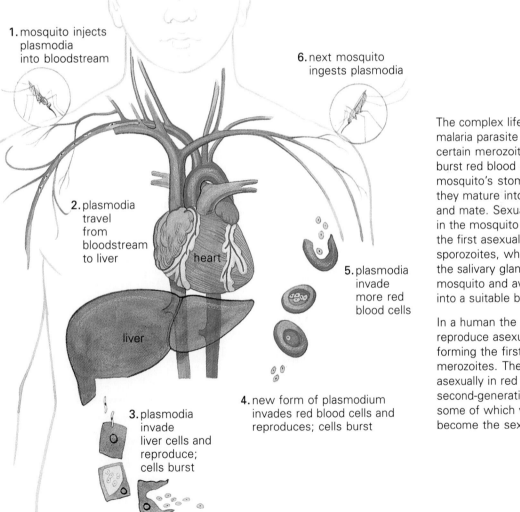

1. mosquito injects plasmodia into bloodstream

6. next mosquito ingests plasmodia

2. plasmodia travel from bloodstream to liver

heart

5. plasmodia invade more red blood cells

liver

3. plasmodia invade liver cells and reproduce; cells burst

4. new form of plasmodium invades red blood cells and reproduces; cells burst

The complex life cycle of the malaria parasite begins when certain merozoites released by burst red blood cells reach a mosquito's stomach, where they mature into sexual forms and mate. Sexual reproduction in the mosquito is followed by the first asexual life stage, the sporozoites, which migrate into the salivary glands of the mosquito and await injection into a suitable bird or mammal.

In a human the sporozoites reproduce asexually in the liver, forming the first generation of merozoites. These reproduce asexually in red blood cells as second-generation merozoites, some of which will eventually become the sexual forms.

Symptoms your physician may observe: With blood tests a physician would observe that a person with malaria has *anemia,* a reduction in the number of red blood cells. This condition is caused by the destruction of red blood cells as the malaria-causing parasites reproduce. The job of the red blood cells is to carry oxygen to each cell. Without enough oxygen cell respiration is reduced, leaving a person tired and lacking in energy. Also, a person with malaria develops an enlarged spleen, the organ that removes damaged blood cells from the blood.

Treatment options: To treat malaria people are given the drug *chloroquine* in pill form or by injection into muscle to kill the parasites that are in the bloodstream. If the malaria is caused by parasites resistant to this treatment, people are treated with a combination of quinine, pyrimethamine, and antibiotics.

Stages and progress: After the initial bite that introduces the parasite into the bloodstream, the stages and progress of the disease differ depending on which *Plasmodium* species has infected the body. Each species has a slightly different life cycle and thus causes a difference in the length and severity of the attacks of chills and fever. For each species the *Plasmodium* organisms enter the bloodstream and within a few hours get to the liver. The parasites up to this point have had a protective sporelike covering. In the liver each of these spores develops thousands of new cells that are capable of invading red blood cells. When these cells are released into the bloodstream, they enter the red blood cells, mature, and then reproduce. As they reproduce, the red blood cells burst open as the newly formed organisms travel the bloodstream seeking new blood cells. During this phase a person feels the symptoms. A typical bout of malaria may last from one to four weeks. It is common for someone who gets malaria to have it recur over and over again, perhaps over a lifetime.

- The most common form of the disease is *tertian malaria,* usually caused by *Plasmodium vivax.* Typically the chills, fever, and profuse sweating occur every 48 hours.
- *Plasmodium ovale* causes a milder case of malaria characterized by only a few short attacks.
- Another organism, *Plasmodium malariae,* causes *quartan malaria.* Rather than every 48 hours, the attacks come at intervals of 72 hours.

Barking up the right tree: the rain forest cure for malaria

During the Age of Exploration, when Europeans first ventured into South America, many were bitten by infected mosquitoes and developed malaria. The explorers were treated by the indigenous people, who used bark from certain trees to alleviate the symptoms of the disease. The Europeans named the trees *cinchona,* after the Countess of Chinchon, the wife of a seventeenth century viceroy from Peru who was treated with the bark.

Cinchona trees are tropical members of the madder family. The active ingredient in their bark is *quinine,* a word derived from the native Peruvian name for the tree bark extract. Quinine and its related chemicals are effective for treating malaria and reducing fever. These alkaloid drugs have a characteristic bitter taste and are now synthesized in a laboratory rather than made from bark.

- Malaria with overlapping attacks occurs because there is an infection of two kinds of malaria-causing organisms, each with its own life cycle.

- The most severe form is *falciparum* (fal-SIP-uh-ruhm) *malaria*, caused by the *Plasmodium falciparum* protozoan. This form of malaria does not last as long as the others, but it is more life-threatening. It causes mental confusion and anemia as well as an enlarged spleen and stomach pain. If caught early, a person with falciparum malaria can be treated and recover completely. If not, the disease can progress and be fatal. Anemia and loss of fluids (dehydration) may cause death. If falciparum malaria becomes chronic, it can cause *blackwater fever*, a condition of the liver and kidneys in which the patient bleeds internally, passing dark-colored urine.

Prevention: When visiting or living in an area where malaria occurs, certain precautions should be taken. Antimalarial drugs can be administered to prevent its occurrence. Also, mosquito repellent should be applied to the skin and mosquito netting used in sleeping quarters to prevent the bite of an infected mosquito. Although scientists have worked on developing a vaccine against malaria, none has so far proven useful. This is because as the parasite goes through its different life stages, it changes the chemical makeup of its cell coat. A vaccine with antibodies to fight one stage of the organism cannot fight another stage because the protein coat of each stage is different.

Sickle-cell trait offers protection from malaria

Many Africans and African-Americans carry the genetic trait for sickle-cell anemia. In parts of tropical Africa a large percentage of the population carries the trait. This would seem quite unusual given that if a person gets the trait from both parents, it usually causes a fatal blood disease. But having just one copy of the trait seems to lower a person's chances of getting malaria. Although a person who inherits the trait from one parent does not get sickle-cell disease, some of the red blood cells do show the sickle-cell characteristic. In 1953 scientists first noticed that the trait for sickle-cell anemia seemed to occur more frequently in places where there was a high incidence of falciparum malaria. How could the two facts be related?

"Sickled" red blood cells have irregular, crescent shapes rather than round shapes. They are also rigid and tend to block blood vessels, causing anemia. However, if a red blood cell is infected with a malaria parasite, the cell sickles more readily, then dies, killing the parasite inside it before it can reproduce. The body's immune cells have a better chance of getting rid of the remaining disease-causing organisms before a full-blown case of malaria develops. So in tropical locations, sickled blood cells actually provide a defense against malaria.

Mal du mer	*See* **Seasickness**
Malignancies	*See* **Cancers**
Manic depressive syndrome	*See* **Bipolar disorder**

Marfan's syndrome

DISEASE

TYPE: GENETIC

See also
Aneurysm
Arteries
Circulatory system
Eyes and vision
Genetic diseases
Heart
Scoliosis

✳ People who are affected by *Marfan's syndrome* have a defect in one of the proteins that are the main building blocks of the body's cells. The protein, called *fibrillin*, is especially abundant in such tissues as bones, ligaments, major blood vessels, and valves of the heart. When fibrillin is scanty or its structure is faulty, a wide variety of signs and symptoms may appear.

The most visible effects are those that involve the bones and joints. A person with Marfan's syndrome is often unusually tall, with long arms and legs and "spidery" fingers. The face may be narrow, with a high-arched palate (roof of the mouth) and crowded teeth. The joints are likely to be exceptionally loose, particularly in the hands and wrists. The spine may twisted out of line (*scoliosis*), and the breastbone may either bulge forward or form a sunken valley between the ribs.

The eyes are often affected. The lens of the eye, for example, is held in place by ligaments. Fibrillin deficiency may weaken ligaments so that the lens can slip off center, a condition called *ectopia lentis* ("displacement of the lens"). The defect does not cause blindness, but it does make vision less sharp. *Nearsightedness* (myopia) is another common problem.

Even more common and more potentially serious are effects on the heart valves, which normally keep the blood flowing in a single direction through the heart. One or more of these valves may not close properly, so that some of the blood leaks backward rather than moving forward. The heart must then work harder than it should to make up for the diminished flow, and it tends to become overenlarged, with a risk of eventual failure.

Most dangerous of all is a weakening of the body's largest artery, the aorta, just above the point where it leaves the heart. Blood is pumped through this part of the aorta at high pressure; when its walls are weakened by fibrillin deficiency, they may bulge outward to form an *aneurysm*. A sudden, large split can cause death from massive internal bleeding.

Causes: The gene responsible for the formation of fibrillin has been traced to chromosome 15, and its long chain of DNA has been analyzed. Marfan's syndrome can apparently result from any one of a large number of possible mutations in the gene. The wide range of these mutations may account for the wide range of physical effects that the condition produces.

Marfan's syndrome is produced by a dominant gene (see Genetic diseases). It is most often inherited from an affected parent. About a quarter of all cases, however, result from some new mutation either in the father's sperm or the mother's egg. Moreover, a mildly affected parent can have a severely affected child, a severely affected parent can have a mildly affected child, brothers and sisters can be affected to different degrees, and so forth.

Incidence: Marfan's syndrome is believed to affect about 1 in 10,000 people in the United States. That figure may be low, since some of those who have the condition have never been diagnosed with it.

Symptoms you are likely to notice: The observable signs of Marfan's syndrome vary widely. They are seldom apparent at birth, and they may not become recognizable until adolescence or adulthood, if then. Sometimes they are so mild that they go completely unnoticed.

Symptoms your physician may observe: Outward signs of Marfan's syndrome, such as skeletal changes or vision blurred by displaced lenses, are less common than internal signs such as a faulty heart valve or a weakened aorta. Blood leaking backward through a valve defect, for example, may cause a heart murmur, audible through a stethoscope.

Still, the condition sometimes escapes detection. The potential dangers of undiagnosed Marfan's syndrome were graphically demonstrated by the sudden deaths of college basketball star Chris Patten in 1977 and Olympic volleyball player Flo Hyman in 1986. Neither of them knew that they had inherited this condition.

Theoretically it should be possible to use DNA analysis in a family with a history of Marfan's syndrome in order to establish which members are affected, regardless of whether they show signs or symptoms. Such testing should identify specific gene mutations in an affected fetus or baby or in a parent with

Did Lincoln have Marfan's syndrome?

He was tall, thin, and loose-jointed. His arms and legs were unusually long. He had big hands and feet, and his fingers were long and slender. Some medical experts think that Abraham Lincoln had Marfan's syndrome. If so, and if he had not been assassinated, he still might have died relatively young from heart failure or a burst aorta.

no symptoms. At present, however, such testing is not usually performed. Instead, when a family history of the disorder is known, a child may be carefully and repeatedly examined for its telltale signs so that treatment can start as soon as possible.

Treatment options: Early treatment can help head off at least some of the harmful effects of the disorder. Physical therapy, a supportive brace, or surgery can be used to correct spinal deformation. Orthodontics can widen the jaw and allow more room for crowded teeth. Glasses can improve weakened vision.

But the most important forms of treatment are intended to minimize the risks of heart and aorta damage. Individuals with the disorder are advised to avoid strenuous exercise and heavy exertion, which raise the blood pressure. They may also be given medicines that reduce blood pressure. Since their heart valves are especially susceptible to infections they are given preventive antibiotics whenever they undergo any medical treatment (including dental treatment) that might penetrate blood vessels. In severe cases surgery may be needed to repair or replace a faulty heart valve. When the aorta is greatly enlarged, a synthetic tube may be surgically inserted to replace the damaged section.

Outlook: Early detection and treatment make this condition far less dangerous than it was just a couple of decades ago. Nevertheless, the risks of heart failure or aorta rupture cannot be entirely eliminated. Life expectancy is lower than usual.

Mast cells   *See* **Phagocytes and other leukocytes**

Mastoiditis   *See* **Earache**

Measles (rubeola)

DISEASE

TYPE: INFECTIOUS (VIRAL)

✳ *Measles* is a very contagious disease caused by a virus. Prior to 1963, when the first measles vaccine became available, large outbreaks occurred almost every year. Sometimes so many children were ill that elementary schools were closed until the outbreak was over.

Cause: The measles virus is passed from person to person by exhaled droplets from the nose and throat. This disease goes by many different names: red measles, hard measles, nine day measles, and rubeola.

Incidence: Until the 1960s about 90% of the population had measles by the age of 20. The development of a vaccination for measles and requirements that children be vaccinated before entering school have dramatically reduced the incidence. In 1991 there were fewer than 10,000 cases of measles in the United States.

Symptoms you are likely to notice: Measles begins with a fever, cough, and runny nose. This is followed in a few days by a rash of small, slightly raised spots. The rash usually begins on the head and face and moves down the body.

Symptoms your physician may observe: If there are no complications, measles does not require a trip to the doctor; a phone call describing the symptoms is usually enough. A doctor can do a blood test to identify measles, but usually this is not necessary.

Treatment options: Measles is a viral infection. Like most diseases caused by viruses, it must run its course—that is, it cannot be cured by medications, but the immune system will eventually overpower it. Bed rest and keeping the person comfortable are the most effective treatments. Some individuals become sensitive to light and are more comfortable in a darkened room. Some benefit from a humidifier because it makes it easier for them to breathe.

Stages and progress: The first symptoms of measles occur ten to twelve days after infection. During the initial fever, runny nose, and cough, the patient feels miserable. On the third or fourth day the fever drops and tiny white spots appear on the inside of the mouth. Next the fever returns and the itchy rash begins. The rash spreads, the spots get larger, and they run together. After four to seven days the rash begins to disappear and is gone in a day or two.

Most cases of measles, especially those in children, are uncomplicated. Babies and adults with measles have more severe cases and are more likely to experience complications. The most common complication is pneumonia, but inflammation of the brain (*encephalitis*), middle ear infections (*otitis media)*, and *convulsions* can also occur. Because of the possibility of complications, which sometimes can be fatal, measles should never be taken lightly.

See also
Convulsion
Coughs
Encephalitis
Fever
Otitis media
Rashes
Vaccination and disease
Viruses and disease

The danger of complications can be reduced by good observation of symptoms. Talk with the doctor if the sick individual complains of earaches or headaches or if the symptoms linger for more than a week after the rash appears. *If convulsions occur, get medical help immediately.*

Prevention and risk factors: A person infected with measles virus can transmit it to others from about five days before symptoms appear to about five days after they appear. Because measles is very contagious, it is difficult to prevent exposure.

The best prevention for measles is vaccination. The MMR is a vaccine to prevent measles, mumps, and rubella; it is given in two doses. The first dose is given when a child is 12 to 15 months old; the second is given when a child is 4 to 6 years old in preparation for entering school. Most people born before January 1, 1957, have had measles and have natural immunity to the disease. Anyone born after than date needs two doses of MMR vaccine to protect them from measles.

"German" measles (rubella), caused by a different virus, can pose serious risks to the developing fetus of a pregnant woman. Measles (rubeola) does not carry the same risk. If the woman is immunized, she is probably safe in settings where measles might be spread but she should discuss this with her doctor. If an unvaccinated woman is pregnant, she is advised to delay vaccination until after pregnancy.

Effects on world population and health: In the United States and other parts of the industrialized world where immunization is the rule, measles is a relatively minor health problem. The last mini-epidemic of American cases ended in 1993 after 50,000 cases and 132 deaths. But in developing countries measles is still a major cause of death in children. According to the World Health Organization (WHO), more than 1 million children died from measles in 1994.

WHO has a massive immunization effort under way. Its goal is to have 90% of all children worldwide vaccinated against preventable childhood diseases by the year 2000. In Africa these efforts have reached 50% of all children. In some areas 99% of children have been vaccinated against measles, but in other areas only 25% have received measles vaccinations.

If the WHO goal for the year 2000 is reached, measles may join smallpox as an extinct disease.

✳ The rarest form of skin cancer, *melanoma* nevertheless ranks as the most life-threatening of all skin diseases. Doctors can cure most cases when treatment begins before the cancer has become well established; this makes early detection of melanoma especially important. You should familiarize yourself with the characteristic symptoms of melanoma and *do not hesitate to contact your doctor if you have a mole that suddenly changes color or size or becomes irregular in shape.*

There are various types of melanomas, but the most common is *superficial spreading melanoma,* which can occur at any age. About 30% of all melanomas first appear in an existing mole. The rest get started on normal skin, often where the skin is regularly exposed to sunlight.

Causes: Doctors believe the ultraviolet radiation in sunlight is the chief cause of melanoma. Exposure to the light has been found to induce some pigment-producing cells in the skin to become cancerous.

Other possible causes include exposure to X rays or chemical pollution. Heredity is also a factor. Some families tend to have moles that become cancerous. Different ethnic groups have differing susceptibilities.

Incidence: About 34,000 cases of melanoma were reported in the United States during a recent year, and of those 7,200 resulted in deaths. Medical experts report melanoma is on the increase though, the number of cases having doubled in the United States over the past two decades.

Melanoma can strike at any age. Along with the rise in total number of cases, however, doctors have reported they are now seeing melanomas more frequently on younger patients.

Symptoms you are likely to notice: Generally you should be suspicious of any mole that changes size, becomes irregular in shape, swells up or bleeds, itches, or becomes painful. *Consult your doctor as soon as possible after you notice any such symptoms connected with a mole.*

Remember also that melanomas frequently develop on normal skin.

Several different varieties of melanoma have somewhat different appearances.

Melanoma
(mel-uh-NOH-muh)

DISEASE

TYPE: CANCER

See also
Cancers
Moles and freckles
Skin cancers

- *Superficial spreading melanoma* starts as a small, fast-growing, irregularly shaped patch on the skin. The patch may range from flesh colored to black and could be spotted with other colors, including blue, red, purple, and white.

- *Nodular melanoma* appears as a small, shiny bump or growth that is firm to the touch. It usually ranges from pearl white to black in color. The growth may begin bleeding and then not heal completely. This type usually develops when people are between the ages of 20 and 60.

- *Acral lentiginous melanoma* is involved in only about 10% of melanoma cases, but it is the type most likely for people of races other than Caucasian. This form appears as irregularly shaped dark patches on the palms or soles of the feet. It also sometimes causes dark-colored streaks running lengthwise in a fingernail or toenail. But people with dark skin also commonly have harmless dark-colored growths on the feet, hands, and nails. This makes early detection of acral lentiginous melanoma all the more difficult.

- *Lintigo maligna melanoma* usually strikes the elderly and accounts for only about 5% of all melanomas. This type begins as a noncancerous brown spot on the skin; it does not become cancerous for several years.

Symptoms your physician may observe: The shape and colors of a suspected growth will probably be enough for your doctor to visually diagnose it as a melanoma. But a skin biopsy will be necessary to confirm that it is in fact cancerous. Depending on how advanced the melanoma is, your doctor may decide that further testing is needed to determine whether the cancer has spread. This could include a complete physical examination and even a CT scan to look for places where the cancer has spread to other organs.

Treatment options: The accepted way to treat any melanoma is to remove it surgically, along with a margin of healthy skin around it. The larger the melanoma, the larger the margin of healthy skin that must be removed, because there is a greater chance that cancerous cells have spread. The surgeon may perform a skin graft to cover the site where the melanoma was removed to promote healing. If the melanoma has spread to nearby lymph nodes, these probably will also have to be removed.

Depending on the stage of the melanoma, further postoperative treatment, including anticancer drugs, may be called for. Follow-up examinations on a regular basis are necessary because the cancer may reappear.

When melanomas are detected and treated early, treatment is successful in about 85% of cases. Melanoma can be deadly, however. Thicker, more advanced melanomas are harder to treat and the success rate drops off sharply if they have spread beyond the immediate area on the skin. The five-year survival rate for patients with melanoma that has spread to their lymph nodes is 30%.

Stages and progress: Though melanomas often do get started in a mole, about 70% of them appear in otherwise normal skin. The cancer begins in the skin's pigment-producing cells and at first spreads into the surrounding skin. The melanoma then enters a more dangerous stage, in which the growth thickens and spreads downward. Once it reaches the lymph system or circulatory system, the melanoma spreads to other parts of the body and becomes very difficult to cure. Without medical treatment melanoma is fatal.

Prevention and risk factors: Avoiding excessive exposure to sunlight, especially if you have light-colored skin, is the best way to prevent melanomas. Use commercially available lotions that block ultraviolet rays when you plan to be out in the sun for extended periods. Wearing a hat with a broad brim also protects your face and neck from overexposure to the sun.

People with light-colored skin, red or blond hair, or blue eyes tend to be more susceptible to this form of cancer. People with dark-colored skin are less likely to get melanomas.

✳ *Meniere's disease* is a disorder of the inner ear that sometimes leads to permanent deafness. The disease brings on attacks of vertigo (dizziness), nausea, loss of balance, persistent ringing in the ears, and distorted hearing. Attacks come and go, lasting anywhere from a few minutes to hours at a time. Symptoms then disappear for hours, months, or even years. Hearing loss in the affected ear becomes progressively worse over a period of years.

The disease was first described in 1861 by French physician Prosper Ménière.

Meniere's disease
(MAYN-ee-uhrz)

DISEASE

TYPE: UNKNOWN

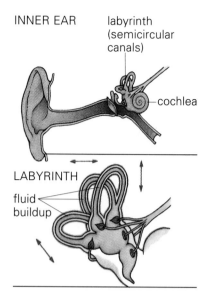

INNER EAR   labyrinth (semicircular canals)

—cochlea

LABYRINTH

fluid buildup

Pressure buildup from fluids in the labyrinth of the inner ear causes the problems with balance and hearing that characterize Meniere's disease.

Causes: Doctors do not know what causes most cases of Meniere's disease. It sometimes develops after a middle ear infection (*otitis media*), a blow to the head, or as a complication of *syphilis*. Whatever the primary cause, the attacks of Meniere's disease increase the pressure of fluids filling part of the inner ear called the *labyrinth*. The body's mechanisms for filtering and excreting the fluid are probably somehow involved. Because of the rising fluid pressure, tissues in the labyrinth are stretched and sometimes torn during attacks, disrupting the patient's hearing and sense of balance.

Incidence: The disease usually strikes men between 40 and 60 years of age, although women may also contract it. One ear is usually affected when symptoms first appear, but anywhere from a quarter to a half of all patients eventually develop the condition in the other ear.

Symptoms you are likely to notice: Though the severity of symptoms may vary, most people with this disorder will eventually suffer attacks of dizziness serious enough to cause nausea, vomiting, and profuse sweating. There may be a sensation of pressure in the ears and usually there is a persistent ringing or buzzing in the ears. Muffled hearing or complete hearing loss in certain frequencies may accompany other symptoms.

Anyone suffering these symptoms for the first time should contact a physician as soon as possible. Unless told to do otherwise, it may be best to lie down and remain as still as possible until the attack subsides.

Symptoms your physician may observe: The doctor will probably conduct tests to determine the frequencies that you are having trouble hearing and the extent of your hearing loss. Another test, called electronystagmography (ee-LEK-troh-ny-stag-MOG-rah-fee), is designed to test the balancing function of the inner ear. Despite it lengthy name, the test is fairly simple. People with a normal, healthy inner ear unconsciously flicker their eyes when water is poured into the ear. The physician studies that flicker of the eyes with a series of tests in which water of different temperatures is poured into your ear. Responses are compared with known normal reactions.

Treatment options: Medications can help relieve symptoms of dizziness and nausea as well as the anxiety that can accompany a severe attack. The physician may also recommend changes in diet, such as avoiding alcohol, cutting back on caffeine, and switching to low-salt foods to help reduce fluid retention.

Surgery to relieve fluid pressure within the inner ear is an option when attacks are severe and other treatments fail. The surgeon may also decide that it is necessary to cut the nerve associated with the balance function.

Stages and progress: Meniere's disease usually begins with attacks in one ear but later affects the other in anywhere from a quarter to a half of the cases. The attacks of dizziness and nausea come and go with varying degrees of frequency and severity. There is a gradual loss of hearing in the affected ear over a period of a few years, but the symptoms sometimes disappear before it becomes complete.

Prevention: Until doctors discover the cause for Meniere's disease, it will be impossible to say what can be done to prevent it. Taking reasonable precautions against head injuries and seeking prompt treatment of ear infections will help eliminate these two potential causes of Meniere's disease.

See also
Balance
Deafness
Dizziness
Nausea
Syphilis
Tinnitus

Hearing aids

About 5 million Americans wear hearing aids and another 20 million could enjoy significantly improved hearing with them. Most people wear the type that fits directly in the ear canal, but those with more severe hearing loss may get better results with the behind-the-ear model.

For someone suffering from hearing loss, the first step is usually a visit to the family doctor or a specialist. The physician will administer hearing tests and evaluate the disorder. If the problem is in the outer or middle ear, it may be possible to restore hearing with medications or surgery. Hearing loss caused by problems with the inner ear usually requires some kind of hearing aid, however.

Hearing aids do not fully restore normal hearing and may not help all patients, but in many cases they provide considerable improvement. Patients must learn to adjust to the device, which amplifies all sounds, including background noises. That is because people who have gradually lost hearing over an extended period usually also lose the ability to tune out background noises, such as ringing telephones, passing cars, and slamming doors. So it is usually best to start by wearing the hearing aid in a relatively quiet place. Over time the patient can relearn to focus on just the essential sounds of a conversation, for example, and to filter out other noises.

For people with severe hearing loss a cochlear implant may make it possible to hear sounds, recognize speech, and in a few cases may even help with understanding speech without relying on lip reading. Surgeons first implant an electrode in the inner ear and a tiny receiver under the skin behind the ear. The patient then wears an electronic device that changes sounds into codes and sends them to a small transmitter worn behind the ear. The implanted receiving device picks up signals from the transmitter and feeds them to the electrode in the inner ear. There the patient's auditory nerves receive the electronic signals, which are interpreted as sounds.

Meningitis

DISEASE

TYPE: INFECTIOUS (BACTERIAL
VIRAL, FUNGAL)

See also
**AIDS (acquired immunodeficiency
 syndrome)**
Alcoholism
Bacteria and disease
Brain
Cancers
Headache
Inflammation
Jaundice
Nervous system
Tuberculosis
Viruses and disease

✳ An infant suddenly develops a raging fever and has trouble breathing. The parents rush to a hospital because they suspect the baby has the disease *meningitis,* which, in its bacterial form, can be life-threatening.

Causes: Meningitis is an infectious disease caused by a variety of microorganisms, including several kinds of bacteria, viruses, and fungi. The disease-causing organisms can spread from person to person by droplets in the air.

Incidence: In the United States *bacterial meningitis* affects about 2,000 to 5,000 young people each year, 70% under the age of five. In adults bacterial meningitis occurs with higher frequency in *alcoholics.* Meningitis is associated with the spread of some kinds of *cancer.* It occurs more frequently in people whose immune system has been damaged by chemotherapy or *AIDS.* One type of bacterial meningitis, *tuberculous meningitis,* affects young children in places where the respiratory disease *tuberculosis* is common.

Viral meningitis is far less serious and may clear up in a week or two. Viral meningitis occurs most often in winter, affecting 9,000 to 12,000 young people in the United States yearly.

Symptoms you are likely to notice: In older children and adults the first symptoms may be severe *headache,* stiffness of the neck and upper back, and mental confusion, followed by fever, vomiting, skin rash, and then convulsions leading to loss of consciousness. In young children, fever, vomiting, restlessness, and decreased levels of energy may be signs. Infants may develop symptoms very quickly and may have a fever, diarrhea, difficulty in breathing, and uncontrolled convulsions. They may also show a yellowing of the skin called *jaundice* and a bulging of the soft spot in the skull. *Anyone experiencing these serious symptoms should immediately seek medical help.*

Symptoms your physician may observe: A physician can test for meningitis by taking a *spinal tap,* a sample of spinal fluid drawn from the lumbar region of the spine. The blood from the fluid is tested and a culture is made.

Treatment options: A diagnosis of bacterial meningitis requires immediate treatment with antibiotics, usually given intravenously in a hospital. Early detection and prompt treatment are crucial and can make the difference between full recovery and severe illness or even death. Mild cases of viral meningitis do not require hospitalization but should be treated with bed rest and any prescribed medications.

Stages and progress: Meningitis occurs when there is an infection somewhere in the body such as in the sinuses or in the *mastoids*, the cavities around the ear. The disease-causing organisms then travel through the bloodstream to the *meninges* and cause a secondary, more serious, infection. The meninges are the three layers of protective membranes that line the spinal cord and the brain. Meningitis, an inflammation of the meninges, may come on quickly or gradually depending on the cause. Bacterial meningitis comes on suddenly and progresses rapidly if untreated. It is fatal in about 15% of cases—significantly higher in infants and adults over 60. Before the days of antibiotics meningitis was more likely to be fatal; it left survivors blind, deaf, or mentally retarded. Even today with antibiotics, some people who recover suffer some permanent brain damage.

Prevention: Because of the variety of disease organisms, vaccines against meningitis are of limited use and offer protection for only a short time. Preventive doses of antibiotics are sometimes given to those in close contact with someone who has developed meningitis. To prevent infection avoid contact with anyone with the disease.

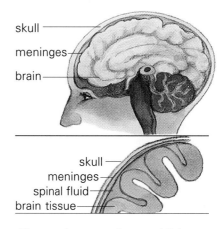

The meninges are layers of lining that help protect the brain and spinal column. But if they become inflamed and swell from an infection, they can cause serious damage to the central nervous system.

✳ *Menstrual pain* consists of the abdominal cramplike aching (with possible nausea, headache, backache, weakness, irritability, and depression) that accompanies menstruation in a woman. It normally occurs at the approximate monthly intervals of menstruation.

Its scientific name is *dysmenorrhea* (dis-MEN-uh-ree-uh). Two main types are recognized. Primary dysmenorrhea is a natural process that is a normal part of menstruation. Secondary dysmenorrhea has an additional underlying cause due to disease or other malfunction.

Cause: The exact cause of menstrual pain remains unknown. The primary type is thought to result mainly from contractions

Menstrual pain

SYMPTOM

of the uterus similar to but weaker than those that occur during childbirth. Such contractions are triggered by a hormonelike chemical, prostaglandin, that is produced with menstruation. It is believed that either production of prostaglandin or sensitivity to it varies among women and that such variation may explain why severity of menstrual pain differs among women.

Secondary dysmenorrhea appears during the menstrual cycle but is caused in most cases by infection, inflammation, or other disorder of the woman's reproductive organs.

Incidence: Only women develop the menstrual pain of primary dysmenorrhea. All women are subject to it during menstruation, but its effects are slight for some. On the other hand, for an estimated one woman in every ten, the effects are so severe that they require cutting back on regular activities to some extent. Those effects can be avoided entirely by the taking of oral contraceptives.

Normally most women start experiencing menstrual pain in the early teenage years, about two years or more after their periods have begun. Regular recurrence may begin when the cycle of ovulation becomes well established. It may lessen spontaneously starting in about the mid-twenties. Few women experience it after the birth of a first child.

Cases of menstrual pain representing secondary dysmenorrhea are comparatively uncommon.

Symptoms you are likely to notice: Many women who get only mild onslaughts of primary dysmenorrhea typically feel headachy and have a tinge of nausea with vague discomfort and a sense of overfullness of the abdomen. Other women go through moderate to severe attacks. Symptoms of these may include pain as if from cramping in the abdomen that varies from noticeable to very sharp; aching in the lower back; an upset stomach with vomiting; headache; frequent voiding of urine and feces; a feeling of faintness and perhaps actual fainting; and emotional depression. These reactions generally start right before or with menstruation and dissipate in the first day or two of menstruation.

Secondary dysmenorrhea typically differs in duration. It tends to start a few days before menstruation and goes on all through menstruation. Its major symptom is a not very sharp but heavy ache that feels lodged far down in the abdomen.

Symptoms your physician may observe: In cases of secondary dysmenorrhea doctors look for evidence of a disorder of the reproductive organs or other organs in the pelvic area. Among these may be an inflammation or infection of the uterus, Fallopian tubes, or intestines. Such a disorder might also include a cyst or benign tumor. An intrauterine device or IUD that had been inserted into the uterus as a contraceptive may also lead to secondary dysmenorrhea.

Treatment: At least some relief of menstrual pain can be realized simply by reducing stress, exertion, and irritation. Helpful measures include getting increased rest, exercising in moderation, and putting an electric heating pad or hot-water bottle on the stomach. Also helpful for relief is the taking of common pain relievers such as ibuprofen, sometimes in prescription-strength doses.

Difficult cases of primary dysmenorrhea have been found to be relieved for some nine of every ten women by medicines that inhibit the production of prostaglandins. These must be prescribed by a physician and seem to prove most effective when the physician also guides the woman in their use.

Treatment of secondary dysmenorrhea often requires the help of a specialist to diagnose and correct the disorder that is its specific contributing cause.

Prevention: Attacks of menstrual pain tend to be heightened in their intensity if a woman is unusually fatigued or stressed. Making efforts to be as well-rested and stress-free as possible by the expected time of menstruation may hence reduce the customary severity of an attack.

Oral contraceptives or birth control pills suppress ovulation and menstruation. Taking them therefore leaves a woman free of menstrual pain while they are active in her system.

✳ People in the past—and some in certain cultures today—attributed mental illness to possession by demons or other evil spirits. In recent years physicians have learned that for the most serious *mental illnesses*, which are termed *psychoses* (sy-KOH-seez—*psycho-* means "mind"), the demons are most often chemical in nature, although there may also be genetic and environmental factors. Today mental illness is treated by specialists known as *psychiatrists* (sih-KY-uh-trists), who are also

Mental illnesses

REFERENCE

medical doctors, and *psychologists* (sy-KOL-uh-jists), who are not medical doctors.

Cause: Early in the nineteenth century it was generally assumed by physicians that mental illness was the result of a disease of the brain, but this concept lost favor when specific evidence was found lacking—outside of a few known disorders such as syphilis, lead poisoning, and so forth. Also, therapies such as *psychoanalysis* (sy-koh-uh-NAL-us-sis—a specific technique based on theories of Sigmund Freud) began to show some success near the end of the century. At that time it was believed that simply talking about the problem could not make people well if there were a physical condition involved. By the mid-twentieth century the idea of a physical basis for mental illness was rejected by most psychiatrists.

Increasingly, however, modern medicine has found that common mental problems, especially serious mental illnesses, can be traced to chemical imbalances in the brain itself, perhaps with a genetic basis in some instances. Recently it has been shown that talking by itself can change brain chemistry, disposing of that objection to a physical cause for mental disease. The main proof of the theory that most major mental illnesses are caused by or at least influenced by the production of various chemicals in the brain, however, is that drugs that change the levels of those chemicals in the brain relieve symptoms. Furthermore, brain-imaging techniques show that chemicals such as amphetamines can be observed mediating brain responses while a person is solving a puzzle.

Less serious mental illness of the type termed *neuroses* (noo-ROH-seez) may or may not have a cause rooted in biochemistry or genetics; but often the anxieties and fears of neuroses can be reduced with chemical medication. (The prefix *neuro-* is used to mean the nervous system but in this case it is used in the sense of "nerves," meaning jumpiness and a vague ill feeling.)

Recognizing mental illness: One of the main problems physicians and therapists face when dealing with mental illness is that it is very difficult to diagnose. The patient may want to hide symptoms instead of describing them, or may be too confused about reality to be able to differentiate between symptoms of mental illness and ordinary thought. Furthermore, different mental illnesses may have similar symptoms, just as different infectious diseases can produce a fever and a rash. The American Psychiatric Society's *Diagnostic and Statistical Manual of Mental Disorders* is published in an effort to help physicians to solve this difficult problem. The *DSM*, as it is known, is hundreds of pages long. The brief paragraphs that follow give only very general descriptions. In many cases more details on specific mental illnesses are provided in separate entries.

Mental illnesses can be grouped in several ways. Certain disorders are the result of specific diseases that cause *dementia*, the medical term for severe confusion and forgetfulness. These include *Alzheimer's disease* and *Creutzfeldt-Jakob disease*. Ingestion or injection of chemicals can produce many mental symptoms and the *DSM* lists the various forms of *alcoholism* and *drug abuse* as mental illnesses. The complex disease known as *schizophrenia* and several diseases similar to it are hard to classify, so they get their own listings; these diseases come closest to the common image of "madness." Various forms of depression and mania, including *bipolar disorder* and *clinical depression*, are grouped with less severe depressions as "mood disorders." Another large group of mental illnesses are the "anxiety disorders," which includes *panic attacks* and *obsessive-compulsive disorder.* A group labeled "dissociative disorders" includes both *multiple-personality disorder* and a form of *amnesia.*

Some disorders are less severe, but still clearly problems. These include such sleep disorders as *insomnia* and *impulse control-disorders*—in these a person cannot control bad habits such as stealing or gambling, for example. The group labeled "sexual disorders" in the *DSM* consists partly of behaviors that often lead to illegal acts, such as sex acts with children, and partly of difficulties in having normal sexual relations. The *DSM* also covers conditions that might be considered a poor adjustment to society instead of mental illness.

Incidence: Over a lifetime an American has about a 48% chance of developing a condition that might be characterized as mental illness, provided that such conditions as alcoholism and fear of public speaking are included. If the definition of mental disorder is limited to such serious illnesses as various forms of depression, schizophrenia, or multiple personality disorder, the percentage drops dramatically. The most common mental illness of all is clinical depression, which at 17% in a lifetime is even more common than alcoholism dependence

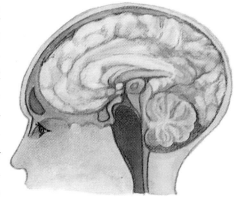

Mental illnesses often involve too much or too little of the neurotransmitters or an incorrect response to them, especially serotonin and dopamine. These chemicals alter moods as they communicate between the cells of the brain.

(14% in a lifetime). Some 13% face phobias in the course of their lives, such as 11% with fear of flying.

Treatment options: Although there may have been some herbal remedies, not much short of confinement was used to treat severe mental disorders before modern times. Less severe problems were often ignored, although biblical accounts tell that King Saul's depression was treated with music. In England in the eighteenth century, facilities and medical attention were instituted for people with "nervous, hypochondriacal, or hysteric diseases" or with "madness" or "feeble-mindedness."

Some early treatments were examples of what today is a sometimes labeled "talking therapy." These include any treatment that consists primarily of either the patient or the doctor talking to the other. Among the first such talking therapies was *hypnosis*, in which the doctor first talks the patient into a receptive state and then either makes suggestions, or has the patient describe feelings, or both. In the late nineteenth century hypnosis evolved into psychoanalysis, the most famous talking therapy. In this type of therapy the patient talks to the doctor about dreams and childhood on a regular basis for long periods of time.

Currently the most popular talking therapies focus on the patient describing immediate problems while the therapist gives small amounts of advice. In numbers, the most popular therapy is group self-help, usually modeled on Alcoholics Anonymous (AA). In group self-help a small number of people who share a specific problem talk mostly about the problem, but also communicate to each other their feelings about life in general. As a treatment method talking therapies of one kind or another have been highly successful with milder neurotic disorders and somewhat less so with addictions. Few pure talking therapies assume a physical basis for the mental disorder being treated (although AA is an exception to this general rule).

Just as tradition has it that a good fright will cure hiccups, some doctors reasoned that disrupting the pathways of the brain might cure incoherent or misdirected thinking. Around 1930 both chemical and electrical shock treatments (ECT, for electroconvulsive therapy) were somewhat successful with both schizophrenia and bipolar disorder. The even more profound shock of removing a part of the brain, called prefrontal lobotomy, was also tried. Except for ECT, which is still used for intractable depression, these violent cures have been almost completely abandoned.

It has long been known that some natural chemicals affect the mind. Shamans (tribal healers) used nicotine or chemicals in mushrooms to induce trance states, for example. Modern chemicals also affect the mind, starting with the first barbiturates in 1863. While barbiturates were tried as a treatment for mental illness, especially in Swiss clinics, they were not very effective. In the 1950s the minor tranquilizers, such as reserpine, and the major tranquilizers, such as thorazine, were introduced. Although these chemicals seemed to relieve stress and anxiety, the early tranquilizers had widespread effects on the body as well, resulting in side effects that limited their use.

The minor tranquilizers were used to combat generalized anxiety and specific phobias. By 1989 more than 36.4 million *new* prescriptions were written for these minor tranquilizers, 81% of them for such drugs as alprazolam (Xanax) and diazepam (Valium). As early as 1964 a significant study by the U.S. National Institutes of Health found that certain major tranquilizers were effective in treating schizophrenia. Lithium compounds for the treatment of bipolar disorder as well as for clinical depression gradually became popular in the early 1970s. Other somewhat effective "psychic energizers" or antidepressants also came into use.

The mid-1980s saw the arrival of a more effective drug for depression too mild to treat with lithium (which has some alarming side effects) and too much a part of the personality to disappear easily with talking therapy. Fluoxetine (trade name Prozac) and similar drugs elevate serotonin, one of the main chemicals used in the brain to signal from one nerve cell to another. For reasons that are poorly understood, higher serotonin levels tend to remove depression and reduce the impulse toward violence in most people. Furthermore, even obsessive-compulsive disorder, previously thought to have no physical basis, often yields to Prozac or other drugs that raise serotonin levels.

In any case, a new age of drugs is dawning. For the first time medicine has been able to understand how the mind works well enough to design specific chemicals that can resolve specific problems. For mental illnesses with poorly understood physical causes, however, the preferred treatment today is drug therapy combined with one or more talking therapies.

Migraine

DISEASE

TYPE: COMBINATION

See also
Circulatory system
Headache

✳ *Migraine* has been known as a special kind of headache ever since ancient times. The name comes from a Greek word meaning "half the head," since migraine headaches often occur, or at least begin, on just one side of the head.

A number of features set migraine apart from other headaches. First, migraine headaches are recurrent—they keep coming back, frequently or infrequently. The average is one to three attacks a month, and attacks tend to be very similar in form.

Unlike other kinds of headaches migraine seems to be at least partly hereditary. About two of three people who get migraine headaches have family members who get them too.

Migraine afflicts more women than men. Female hormones may play a part in triggering attacks or making them more severe. Many women have migraine headaches before or during their menstrual periods, and attacks often taper off after menopause. Some women do not have attacks during pregnancy.

In some people migraine attacks are triggered by emotional stress or by drinking or eating particular things, such as alcohol or foods rich in the amino acid *tyramine*. Most migraine attacks, however, are spontaneous—they just happen.

The pain of a migraine headache has a throbbing quality, and it can be quite intense and disabling. It may start on just one side of the head and then radiate to the rest of the head or into the neck, shoulders, or back.

Bright lights, loud noises, strong odors—any strong stimulation of the senses—tends to make the pain worse. Those suffering an attack typically feel an urge to retreat to a dark, quiet place where they can rest until the pain subsides. Attacks may last anywhere from a few hours to several days—a "sunup to sundown" pattern is common. Headache is often accompanied by a digestive system upset such as nausea, constipation, or diarrhea. That's why migraine is described as a "sick headache."

The majority of sufferers have *common migraine*. But a minority have *classic migraine*. They not only have recurrent headaches but also experience distinctive sensory disturbances—known collectively as an *aura*—before each attack. Bright spots may appear before the eyes, or parts of the visual field may seem blinded. The visual disturbance may be accompanied by "pins and needles" or other abnormal sensations in the skin. The headache begins shortly afterward.

Cause: Migraine is part of a group described as *vascular headaches*. Vascular headaches originate in the blood vessels (the vascular system), specifically in the arteries that carry blood to the head. For reasons not yet understood, these blood vessels suddenly swell, or *dilate*, stimulating pain-sensing nerves nearby. The throbbing quality of the pain corresponds to the pulse of blood being pumped through the arteries.

Incidence: Migraine is very common, especially among women. About 30% of women between the ages of 21 and 35 are believed to suffer from it to some degree.

Symptoms you are likely to notice: Migraine attacks vary among individuals, but they often follow a pattern in a particular individual. They tend to appear about the same time of day and last for about the same length of time. The pain of migraine is distinctive: It throbs at the rate of the pulse.

If you have classic migraine (most sufferers have only the common variety), you may experience the sensory disturbances of an aura about half an hour before an attack begins.

Symptoms your physician may observe: There are no special diagnostic tests for migraine. It is generally diagnosed from the symptoms reported by the sufferer.

Treatment options: Migraine attacks can often be controlled by a combination of medications and lifestyle management techniques. Because stress plays a large part in triggering

Migraine may be triggered by such foods as aged cheese, red wine, or preserved fish, which contain tyramine. Noises and bright lights become almost unbearable after the headache starts.

attacks (as it does in other kinds of headaches), relaxation exercises and other stress-management techniques can be very helpful. Another adjustment in life-style may be the avoidance of alcohol and foods known to provoke attacks.

Relatively mild migraine headaches may be relieved by common painkillers such as acetaminophen (Tylenol), aspirin, and ibuprofen. One widely used drug since 1993 for serious attacks is sumatriptan (trade name: Imitrex), which acts on the serotonin receptors in the brain. It is injected by the patient and in studies relieves 70% of all migraines. The painkiller lidocaine, administered as a nasal spray, is also effective.

Outlook: Migraine attacks tend to become less frequent and less severe over time. Many women stop suffering from them about the time they reach menopause.

Prevention: Certain drugs may be helpful in preventing migraine attacks as well as making them less severe. Among them are propranolol and verapamil, which are ordinarily used to treat high blood pressure and heart disease. Another drug is methysergide, which is taken between attacks rather than at the beginning of an attack. Some success is also reported with antidepressives such as amitriptyline.

Minamata disease

DISEASE

TYPE: CHEMICAL
       ENVIRONMENTAL

See also
Dementia
Environment and disease
Poisoning

✳ In the early 1950s fishers and other villagers around Minamata Bay on Kyushu Island, Japan, began to develop neurological problems. There were also many stillbirths and children born with serious defects. *Minamata disease* gets its name from this outbreak of disease that occurred at that time. Eventually the disease was traced to *mercury poisoning* of fish in Minamata Bay.

Mercury in lakes and the oceans continues to be a major health concern. Mercury that has been consumed in small amounts remains in the tissue of the consumer. When the consumer is later consumed, as when a big fish eats a smaller fish, the mercury is concentrated at a higher level.

Cause: Mercury is dangerous in all forms, as an element and in all compounds, but it is also extremely useful in industrial processes. The exact mode of mercury poisoning is not clear, but it seems likely that mercury removes sulfur from key proteins, making them useless. It also destroys kidney cells.

The mercury poisoning that affected the Minamata population was caused by industrial wastes that had been dumped in Minamata Bay. Fish caught in Minamata Bay in the 1950s had mercury levels 11 times as great as would be permitted today.

Because mercury is toxic to all forms of life, it has frequently been used as an additive to prevent growth of funguses or other organisms. Mercury has also been used widely as a fungicide on crop seeds.

Rain deposits mercury even in remote lakes. Most of the mercury in rainwater comes from air pollution caused by combustion of materials containing mercury. This is released by cement and phosphate plants' incinerators.

Incidence: About 1,000 people in all are thought to have died from the original Minamata disease outbreak. As recently as the early 1990s about 2,000 people living around Minamata Bay continued to suffer from mercury poisoning.

At least 21 U.S. states, 2 Canadian provinces, and Sweden have had to blacklist lakes in which fish have high levels of mercury. Typically, pregnant or nursing women and young children are advised not to eat fish from such lakes, while others are told to limit their consumption. The worst lakes for mercury contamination are small, shallow ones, or lakes newly created by impounding water.

Symptoms you are likely to notice: Mercury causes dementia. From the sixteenth to the twentieth century, fur used to make felt for hats was treated with nitrate of mercury. Before the danger of this procedure became known, hatters often succumbed to mercury dementia; thus the phrase "as mad as a hatter" entered the language and became the basis of Lewis Carroll's Mad Hatter in *Alice in Wonderland*. Even earlier mercury was used by alchemists because gold and silver dissolve in it. Mercury fumes are thought to have caused dementia in alchemists who used it.

Other symptoms include excess saliva, loose teeth and gum disorders, and apparent drunkenness. In acute poisoning there may also be bloody diarrhea.

Symptoms your physician may observe: Severe mercury poisoning leads to kidney failure and death. In slow poisoning there may also be damage to the stomach and intestines.

Treatment options: For acute poisoning one can induce vomiting or try flushing the stomach. Long-term poisoning may be treated with drugs that capture mercury and enable it to be excreted from the body.

Stages and progress: Mercury in water is often converted by bacteria to the compound methylmercury. Methylmercury is much more easily absorbed by living organisms than elemental mercury. In water it moves up the food chain, where it is concentrated in predator fish. Older, and therefore larger, predator fish are especially prized by humans for food. Also, methylmercury tends to accumulate in the parts of fish that people eat, the muscles. Humans who eat these fish, especially young children, can be harmed.

Mitral stenosis and incompetence
(MY-truhl stuh-NOH-suhs)

DISEASE

TYPE: MECHANICAL
(POSSIBLY GENETIC)

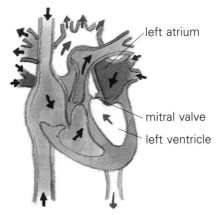

left atrium

mitral valve

left ventricle

Either narrowing of the mitral valve (stenosis) or failure of the valve to work properly (incompetence) eventually produces damage to heart muscle.

✳ *Mitral stenosis* and *mitral incompetence* are separate but similar disorders of the mitral valve of the heart. That valve connects the upper and lower chambers of the left side of the heart. In mitral stenosis the valve is narrower than normal and consequently restricts the passage of blood between the two chambers. This in turn makes the heart work harder to pump blood through the narrowed opening. In mitral incompetence the valve fails to close fully, as it normally should. This allows blood to leak back from one chamber to the other and forces the heart muscle to work harder to pump the additional load of leaked-back blood through the heart.

Mitral incompetence is also termed *mitral insufficiency* or *mitral regurgitation*. It is also a result of a condition termed *prolapse of the mitral valve*. Some individuals have cases of both mitral stenosis and mitral incompetence at the same time.

Causes: *Rheumatic fever*, a complication of infection by *Streptococcus* in childhood or infancy, has traditionally been considered a major cause of either mitral stenosis or mitral incompetence. Scarring of the valve in the course of the fever results in the valve's malfunctioning. However, about half of all those who develop mitral stenosis have no history of rheumatic fever.

Other causes of mitral incompetence include damage to the valve from heart attack or from an incident of heart failure on the heart's left side. An incompetent valve is also thought to be inborn in some cases.

Incidence: For unknown reasons mitral stenosis is developed by some four times as many women as men.

Symptoms you are likely to notice: Getting abnormally out of breath during exertion is one of the first signs of mitral stenosis. Such shortness of breath typically increases until it appears after only very little exertion or even while sitting or lying down. Irregular heartbeats (called palpitations or fibrillation) may also appear. Signs of heart failure such as flushed cheeks, bluish lips, and ankle swelling can also develop. Attacks of coughing that bring up bloodstained mucus may occur as well. Mitral incompetence is also evidenced by shortness of breath and weakness, but these are often less pronounced.

Symptoms your physician may observe: Cardiologists usually diagnose the technical symptoms of these maladies. Such symptoms include the sounds heard through a stethoscope that are popularly called a heart murmur.

Treatment: Medicines including diuretics (to reduce swelling) or digitalis compounds (to counter heart failure) are often prescribed for these diseases. Heart surgery to repair a defective valve or to replace it with an artificial one can remedy the conditions in severe cases.

See also
Arrhythmias
Heart
Heart attack
Heart failure
Palpitations
"Strep"

See **Embryo**

Miscarriage

Moles and freckles

DISEASE

TYPE: GENETIC
CANCER

✳ *Moles* are small, light-to-dark-colored growths on the skin. They are almost always clusters of pigment cells among other skin cells. Nearly everyone has at least some, but people with fair skin tend to have them in greater numbers. *Freckles*—small, flat brown spots—are a common discoloration of the skin caused by exposure to the sun.

Most moles are round, have a clearly defined symmetrical shape, and are smaller than 3/16ths of an inch. They may be flat or raised with color ranges from flesh tones to dark brown or black. Moles rarely pose health problems, but the serious skin cancer *melanoma* sometimes starts in a mole. *Changes in size, color, or shape of a mole may be a sign that a cancer is developing and should be checked by your doctor as soon as possible.*

Babies are sometimes born with another type of skin discoloration, a port wine stain. This reddish purple mark is flat or

See also
Melanoma
Skin
Skin diseases
Warts

just slightly raised and can be quite large. In some cases it may cover as much as half the patient's face. The port wine stain is different from common moles because the skin's pigment cells are not involved in this type of growth. Instead an abnormal cluster of capillaries causes the dark-colored skin. Port wine stains are not cancerous.

Causes: Common moles are clusters of skin pigment cells that begin growing at the point where the outer layer of the skin meets the layer underneath it.

Freckles have a different origin. Heredity figures in the tendency to form them, but the freckle itself initially appears in response to sunlight. When the skin is exposed to sunlight, it produces more melanin, the pigment that gives skin a tan or brown color and helps protect it from sunlight. Pigment cells in fair-skinned children either do not respond to the sunlight or do so unevenly, producing the brown spots we call freckles. While freckles on young children may disappear during the winter, older children and adults with fair skin frequently develop permanent brown spots, called *lentigines* or liver spots, where skin is exposed to the sun.

Incidence: Eventually about 95% of all people develop at least a few moles, and about 1% of people of European descent are born with them. An estimated 5 to 10% of Americans have one or more moles that are what doctors call "atypical." These moles are unusually large and irregularly shaped, or show other signs that they could become cancerous.

Symptoms you are likely to notice: Moles, either raised or flat, that are symmetrical in shape and do not change in size or color usually are no cause for concern, even if you have many of them. But if a mole is growing, becomes irregular in shape, has a mixture of brown, black, or other colors, itches, bleeds, or becomes inflamed or painful, then malignant melanoma may be a possibility. *See your doctor as soon as possible if any of these symptoms develop.*

A doctor should also look at any liver spots that are irregular in shape, uneven in color, or exhibit other unusual symptoms.

Symptoms your physician may observe: Generally, if your doctor is suspicious about an atypical mole, he or she will remove it and have it analyzed to see if cancer cells are present.

Treatment options: Large or atypical moles can be removed surgically, usually in the doctor's office. Giant moles may have to be removed in stages, however, because of their size. If a port wine stain is disfiguring, it may be removed surgically when a child is about three or four years of age.

Liver spots can usually be faded or cleared up with applications for six to ten months of a medication called tretinoin.

Prevention: You cannot prevent moles from growing in the first place, but you should take care to avoid irritating them whenever possible. Where clothing regularly rubs against a mole, having the mole removed might be a good idea, especially if it has become inflamed or swollen.

✳ Young adults between 15 and 30 are more likely than others to get *mononucleosis*. If someone feels ill and extremely tired for several days in a row, mononucleosis may be the cause.

Cause: Mononucleosis is a contagious disease caused by the Epstein-Barr virus (EBV), a type of herpes virus. The disease is spread by contact, usually with the saliva of an infected person.

Incidence: In the United States mononucleosis is most common among young adults of college age. Because it is contagious through infected droplets of saliva, it can be transmitted through kissing and thus is sometimes known as the kissing disease. In less developed parts of world mononucleosis occurs in children as young as two years of age.

Symptoms you are likely to notice: In young children the disease is mild and may go unnoticed. An older child may have a mild sore throat or tonsillitis. Symptoms in young adults are more severe. They may complain of a headache, swollen eyelids, chills, severe fatigue, and loss of appetite. Patients may also run a fever, have a sore throat for several days, and experience swollen glands in the neck, underarms, or groin area for several weeks. There may be difficulty in swallowing, bleeding gums, skin rash, or bruising. A rarer symptom is jaundice, which indicates a problem with liver function.

Symptoms your physician may observe: Because mononucleosis has some symptoms similar to those of "strep" throat, meningitis, "German" measles, appendicitis, and even some

Mononucleosis

DISEASE

TYPE: INFECTIOUS (VIRAL)

See also
Fatigue
Fever
Lymphocytes
Phagocytes and other leukocytes
Spleen
Viruses and disease

forms of cancer, it is important to see a physician. A physical examination and a blood test will confirm the disease.

By examining a blood sample, a physician can see the abnormally large number of *mononuclear* white blood cells that are circulating through the bloodstream (this is how the disease gets its name). White blood cells have a nucleus, unlike red blood cells, which lack them entiely. Since the job of white blood cells is to fight disease, a large number of thcm suggcsts that the immune system is hard at work. Other symptoms a physician may detect are signs of an enlarged spleen, which occurs in 50% of cases, or an enlarged liver, which occurs in 20%.

Treatment options: Treating mononucleosis has changed somewhat in recent years as physicians learn more about the virus that causes it. In the past bed rest for four to six weeks and limited activity for several months was recommended. Today, however, physicians prescribe a shorter bed rest period, from six to ten days, and anticipate full recovery in four to six weeks. However, doctors recommend avoiding strenuous exercise to prevent damage to the spleen if it has become enlarged with the infection.

Home care includes relief of symptoms such as gargling with salt water to soothe a sore throat. Fluids to prevent dehydration and a nutritious diet are also important. To relieve pain, over-the-counter pain relievers such as acetaminophen (for example, Tylenol) can be taken. However, *children and teenagers should not take aspirin because of the risk of Reye's syndrome,* a potentially harmful condition of the nervous system and liver.

Antibiotics do not work to kill the Epstein-Barr virus or any other virus. However, people with mononucleosis sometimes also develop *"strep" throat,* and antibiotics are used to kill the streptococcus bacteria that causes it. Most people recover fully from mononucleosis without complications.

Stages and progress: Symptoms of mononucleosis may appear four to six weeks after exposure to the Epstein-Barr virus and progress may vary with the person. The greatest danger of going without treatment is a ruptured spleen.

Prevention: Avoid close contact with a person who has mononucleosis. Keep immunity up by getting enough rest. If you do get the disease, it imparts immunity for life.

Traveling by car, train, airplane, or boat sometimes causes *motion sickness,* an unpleasant feeling of dizziness accompanied by headache, nausea, and in more severe cases, vomiting. In almost all cases the discomfort disappears with no lasting effects once the trip is over.

Causes: Problems with motion sickness begin in the inner ear. The inner ear has three fluid-filled semicircular canals that sense balance when you are walking or standing upright. Horizontal motion—walking, for example—often has no adverse effect because the semicircular canals are used to the stimuli produced by it. But vertical motion, such as that experienced on a bumpy plane flight or even during a ride in an elevator, is another matter. The sudden rise or fall stimulates the semicircular canal into a feeling of falling.

Though vertical motion is the cause of much motion sickness, other factors also enter in. The different signals that reach your brain from your eyes and from your balance organs in the ear may be a part of the problem. Some, for example, experience motion sickness if they stare at a fixed object in a vehicle. Such people cannot read while riding in a car or train, although the smoother motion and more complete enclosure of an airplane may produce no motion sickness.

If you are emotionally distressed, perhaps because of anxiety about a trip, you may be more likely to get motion sickness. In fact, some people who have suffered air sickness previously get so anxious about traveling that they get sick before the plane has even taken off.

Other things can make you more likely to get motion sickness as well. Going hungry or eating a heavy meal before traveling may lead to airsickness. Lack of fresh air, tobacco smoke, and unpleasant odors also contribute to motion sickness.

Incidence: While only a small fraction of people who travel by car, train, or air suffer motion sickness, the problem is not uncommon.

Symptoms you are likely to notice: A mild case of motion sickness may involve nothing more than dizziness, headache, and a queasy feeling in the stomach. Severe motion sickness can be quite debilitating though. People may vomit uncontrol-

Motion sickness

INJURY

TYPE: MECHANICAL

Space sickness

Some of the most severe motion sickness occurs in space capsules that orbit the earth, including U.S. space shuttle flights. It is not the great speed of about 20,000 mph that causes this form of motion sickness. In a way, it is the absence of a sensation of motion.

People in an orbiting satellite are in a state of free fall, also known as weightlessness. Every part of the spaceship is falling toward earth as it also speeds forward. The combined motions produce the elliptical path that keeps a satellite in orbit.

The semicircular canals register that the space traveler is falling toward earth. But the eyes report that the traveler is stationary in the cabin of the spaceship. At first space travelers often feel intense motion sickness, especially nausea. After a while the brain retrains itself to ignore the signals of falling that are coming from the inner ear. The orbiting traveler's space sickness ends. But there will be another period of adjustment to come when the traveler returns to earth.

lably and be unable to keep fluids or foods down. They turn pale, their skin becomes cold and clammy, and, weakened by the vomiting and dizziness, they may find it hard to remain standing or even sitting upright.

Treatment options: If medication is needed, your doctor may recommend sedatives or antihistamines such as dimenhydrinate (Dramamine), promethazine, or meclizine for use before and during a trip.

Prevention: For severe or persistent motion sickness the best approach is to take preventive medicine before traveling.

You can help prevent mild carsickness by keeping a window open and by stopping frequently. Take short walks outside during the stops. While riding in the car, you can help relieve the queasy feeling by looking down at the inside of the car. Lying down may also help. Such remedies are not available to the air traveler. When traveling by airplane, eat only small meals that are easy to digest. Reclining your seat and closing your eyes also helps some instances of mild motion sickness.

Mountain sickness

See **Polycythemia**

Multiple myeloma
(MY-uh-LOH-muh)

DISEASE

TYPE: CANCER

✳ *Multiple myeloma* is a cancer of certain white blood cells found in bone marrow and in connective tissue. These cells, known as *plasma cells*, are formed in the red marrow as are some other types of white blood cells. Plasmas cells, which are fewer in number than the more familiar white blood cells that circulate in the blood and lymph, ordinarily function as part of the body's immune system, creating antibodies against infection. Although they are technically white blood cells, few are found in the blood. They are closely related to the B lymphocytes (see Lymphocytes).

When the plasma cells reproduce in abnormal numbers and forms to produce multiple myeloma, they seriously harm several body functions. First, they interfere with the production of red blood cells, causing anemia, and of platelets, impairing blood clotting. The cancer also injures the bones where it is found, especially the flat bones such as ribs, eroding them and making them susceptible to fracture. Finally, the abnormal cells do not produce normal antibodies, so that the body's immune system is weakened.

Cause: The cause of abnormal reproduction of plasma cells is unknown.

Incidence: Multiple myeloma is relatively rare, occurring in 1 in 25,000 people. It is somewhat more common among men than women and occurs most often among people over 40.

Symptoms you are likely to notice: The fatigue and breathlessness typical of anemia are possible, but the most common symptom is pain in the bones, particularly those in the back. Sometimes the bones of the upper and lower jaws are attacked, causing the teeth to become loose in their sockets. General resistance to infection is lowered.

Symptoms your physician may observe: The first sign of the disease is often anemia revealed in a routine blood test. Multiple myeloma is further diagnosed with the help of urine tests and X rays. A common condition caused by the disease is abnormal curving of the spine.

Treatment options: The bone pain is treated with painkillers ranging from aspirin to opiates. Antibiotics may be given to help replace lost immune functions and steroids to reduce inflammation.

   The production of abnormal plasma cells is attacked with the same methods used for other forms of cancer—chemotherapy (anticancer drugs) and radiation. These techniques are potentially harmful to all cells, but they are most destructive to cells that reproduce especially fast, such as cancer cells.

Outlook: The progress of the disease can be slowed down by treatment, but it is eventually fatal, often as a result of infection or bleeding.

Multiple-personality syndrome

DISEASE

TYPE: MENTAL

✳ A patient with *multiple-personality syndrome* has two or more different identities that behave and react differently from each other. Each separate set of responses, temperaments, and often memories is called a *personality*. People with over 20 distinct personalities have been reported. Usually one personality, called the *primary*, is dominant much of the time, but any one of the other *secondary* personalities is capable of taking over.

   Domination by the secondary personality then is so complete that the patient may talk in a different voice, have a dis-

See also
Mental illnesses

tinctly different viewpoint from that of the primary personality or another secondary one, and exhibit markedly different mannerisms and other behavior patterns. In some cases the patient's different personalities even register differently on an electroencephalograph, a device that records electrical activity in the brain.

When the primary personality again comes back into control, it often has no knowledge of what happened while the secondary personality was in control, or "executive," and may be completely unaware that other personalities exist. The secondary personalities are usually aware of the primary personality, however. Multiple-personality patients are attempting to separate conflicting desires and develop distinct personality roles for each—say, a quiet, studious personality and an outgoing, life-of-the-party personality. One or the other personality dominates at any one time.

Cause: Multiple-personality disorder is an extremely exaggerated form of the normal personality conflicts and role variations all people experience. For example, you might want to go to a party and have a good time with friends, but you know you have to study for a test instead. You resolve the conflict by choosing between your desires and either studying for the exam or going to the party and taking the consequences.

Many people who have studied this disease believe that physical abuse, sexual abuse, or other severe emotional or physical trauma during childhood can heighten normal internal conflicts and lead to multiple-personality disorder. Physical or sexual abuse from a parent or other family member, for example, can arouse intense feelings of fear and anxiety in a child. Coping with those emotions can be extremely difficult, and avoiding the emotional conflict altogether may seem to be the only alternative. Multiple-personality patients have done that, experts think, by separating conflicting emotions into different personalities.

Incidence: Once thought to be extremely rare, multiple-personality disorder has been diagnosed more frequently in the United States since publication of a best-selling book, *The Three Faces of Eve,* in 1957. It is still a relatively uncommon disorder, though, and reportedly continues to be misdiagnosed as schizophrenia or as some other mental disorder (because the word *schizophrenia* is often explained as "split personality," there is a common misconception that multiple personality disorder is a form of schizophrenia).

Women suffer this illness more often than men.

Symptoms you are likely to notice: All of us at one time or another do things that seem completely out of character. But with the person suffering multiple-personality disorder, the change from one set of behaviors to another is surprisingly complete and at times even the exact opposite of the person's "normal" responses. Secondary personalities may adopt different styles of clothing, different habits such as smoking or drinking alcohol, and different ways of speaking, as well as a host of changed personality traits. Sometimes secondary personalities in adults even mimic those of young children or members of the opposite sex.

Treatment options: Therapists use hypnosis and psychotherapy to help make the primary personality aware of the secondary personality. At the same time, the patient is taught that having conflicting needs and wants is part of being human, and that too much self-criticism can be harmful.

As the primary personality accepts the existence of other personalities, the patient also becomes aware of the repressed needs, abuse, or other traumas that gave rise to them. This awareness ends the emotional need to maintain other personalities and allows the patient to reintegrate his or her personality into a normal, single identity.

Stages and progress: Although multiple-personality disorder is far from being completely understood, it is most often thought to be an emotional defense mechanism that patients have developed during childhood. For a child emotions can be overwhelming when trying to deal with abuse, severe trauma, or impulses that have been punished harshly. The child may respond by separating—or *dissociating*—those feelings into a part of his or her personality that can be ignored. Emotional walls develop as the need to block out this aspect of the personality continues, and the dissociated part becomes the basis for a separate personality, unknown to the primary personality. Eventually, though, the secondary personality becomes strong enough to take control at times and act out the repressed hate, aggressiveness, or promiscuous behavior.

The Three Faces of Eve

Most people today have at least heard about multiple-personality disorder through various newspaper articles, best-selling books, movies, or sensationalized accounts. Multiple personality disorder has even figured in highly publicized criminal trials for rape and murder. Until the 1950s, though, the disorder was considered so rare and so bizarre that it was of interest only to the psychiatric community.

An Augusta, Georgia, housewife named Eve White changed all that. Entering psychotherapy to cure headaches and fainting spells, the quiet, shy, self-controlled mother of one soon revealed first one and then other secondary personalities. One was Eve Black, a sensuous, sexually adventurous personality that was very much the opposite of Eve White, the primary personality.

Eve White's case first became famous within the psychiatric community in 1954, when her therapists published a paper on her in the *Journal of Abnormal and Social Psychology*. Three years later mainstream America learned of this strange disorder when Eve became the subject of the popular book *The Three Faces of Eve*. The book and an Oscar-winning movie that followed made Eve the first, but by no means the last, of the highly publicized cases of multiple personality.

Multiple sclerosis

(skluh-ROH-sis)

DISEASE

TYPE: AUTOIMMUNE

See also
ALS (amyotrophic lateral sclerosis)
Autoimmune diseases
Nerves
Nervous system
Viruses and disease

✳ *Multiple sclerosis (MS)* is a serious disease that affects nerves in various parts of the body. Usually the disease begins with mild symptoms such as numbness or weakness in an arm or leg. These almost always clear up by themselves, and many people experience no further problems.

For some, however, the episodes continue, appearing sporadically months or even years apart. Between attacks the MS goes into remission (the symptoms disappear), but eventually the chronic flare-ups cause permanent, disabling nerve damage. Depending on the severity of their attacks, MS sufferers may continue to lead relatively normal lives for up to 20 or 30 years after the disease first appears.

In the rare and most severe form of MS, the disease progresses steadily after it first appears and does not go into remission. Thus permanent nerve damage and serious disability occur much sooner with this form of MS.

Cause: Doctors do not know exactly what causes the ordinary form of MS, but they suspect that a virus—adenovirus 2, one cause of the common cold—plays an important role. Some experts believe the initial viral infection may occur during childhood. However, most of those infected do not ever contract MS, and for those that do develop the disease symptoms do not appear until many years after the infection. Thus there may be genetic and environmental factors involved as well.

The viral disease does not damage nerves directly. The patient's immune system does that by its response to the virus. People who develop MS have an inherited immune response to the virus. This response causes their bodies to mistakenly produce antibodies that actually attack the nerves.

The whole nerve is not involved. Instead the antibodies attack the insulating sheath, which is made from a white, fatty tissue called *myelin* (MY-uh-lin). Proteins from adenovirus 2 have amino acid sequences that are remarkably like those of proteins in the myelin sheaths that cover nerves. During an attack of MS the antibodies cause myelin to become swollen and inflamed. This interferes with transmission of nerve impulses along the affected nerve pathway. A thickened patch of damaged tissue is called a *sclerosis* by physicians, so a disease characterized by many such patches is known as "multiple sclerosis." Repeated attacks eventually cause the myelin to break down and disappear in places, permanently damaging the nerve. Among the places most likely to be affected are the nerve cells in the brain and spinal column.

The geographical distribution of the disease suggests that there is an environmental factor at work. One theory is simply that it occurs most often in regions where people frequently experience the common cold and therefore adenovirus 2.

There is also an inherited form of multiple sclerosis, a genetic disease that has the same symptoms as ordinary multiple sclerosis. Inherited MS occurs with a frequency that is about 2 to 3% of the autoimmune disease.

Incidence: MS is more common in temperate zones than in the tropics and subtropics. Women are slightly more likely to get the disease than men. The actual extent of MS is difficult to estimate, however, because mild cases may not even be reported to doctors and may be misdiagnosed when they are. One estimate is that 350,000 Americans have the disease.

Usually MS patients suffer their first attack between the ages of 20 and 40 years old.

Symptoms you are likely to notice: The disease usually begins with tingling, numbness, or weakness in an arm or leg, or in one spot somewhere else on the body. If an arm is affected, you may drop items more often than normal because your muscles are unexpectedly weak. If it is a leg, you may sometimes drag your foot. You may experience temporarily blurred or double vision, move unsteadily, slur words, and have difficulty with urination.

Whatever symptoms occur, they almost always clear up without treatment after a few days or weeks. *Any one of these symptoms is serious enough to warrant medical attention, however, and you should see your doctor as soon as possible.*

Symptoms your physician may observe: MS is capable of producing a wide range of symptoms depending on which nerves have become inflamed. This makes diagnosis of the disease difficult, for other neurological disorders may also cause some of the same symptoms.

An MRI (magnetic resonance imaging) scan may help pinpoint areas of damage to nerves, and blood tests may help doctors eliminate other possible disorders, such as vitamin deficiencies and vascular inflammations, that could cause similar symptoms. A sample of the patient's cerebrospinal fluid will probably also be tested for a telltale protein in the fluid.

Treatment options: No cure for MS exists at this time, although a number of experimental treatments are being researched. The drug beta interferon has been shown to slow the course of MS, and in the mid-1990s a form of beta interferon (Betaseron) became the first drug approved by the U.S. Federal Drug Administration that can actually alter the course of the disease in some patients. Interferons are chemicals normally produced by the immune system; they are part of the vast interlocking mechanism designed to repel foreign substances, such as viruses and cancer. Beta interferon modulates a response involved in the immune attack on the myelin sheath.

When patients have trouble talking or walking during an attack, corticosteroid drugs or corticotropin help control these symptoms. Doctors may also prescribe medication to control problems with spastic muscle movement and with bladder control problems associated with MS.

Counseling and group therapy also can be an important part of treatment. The National Multiple Sclerosis Society maintains chapter offices in many locales. Staff workers provide information and guidance for MS patients and their families.

Stages and progress: For those patients with the pattern of recurring MS and remission, recovery may be almost complete after each of the early episodes. But over time repeated attacks cause cumulative damage to the patient's nerves, resulting in less complete recovery and finally permanent nerve damage. Although it may take many years, MS patients eventually suffer progressive weakness of the arms and legs, loss of vision, or other problems.

Prevention: About 70% of those diagnosed with MS continue to live relatively normal lives five years or more after being diagnosed with the disease. Most persons with MS must make adjustments in the way they live, however. They can help prevent new episodes of disease symptoms by following an exercise and diet regimen designed for general good health. It helps to avoid overexertion, emotional stress, extremes of heat and cold, and sources of infection. In this way most people with MS continue to lead productive lives for many years.

Index

A

Abdominal wall defects 2:70
Abruptio placentae 7:9
Abscess 1:13, 3:108, 7:29
Achilles tendon 8:41
Achlorhydria 8:17
Achondroplasia.
  See Short stature
Acne 1:14-15
Acoustic neuroma 3:28
Acral lentiginous melanoma 5:84
Acromegaly 4:86
ACTH (adrenocorticotropic hormone) 4:84
Actinomycetes 1:88
Actinomycosis 3:108
Acute lymphocytic leukemia 5:57, 5:58, 5:59
Acute nonlymphocytic leukemia 5:57, 5:59
Acute porphyrias 7:1-2
Acute pyelonephritis 5:32-33
Acyclovir 2:60
ADA deficiency 2:16-17, 4:108
Addiction 3:34, 3:36
Addison's disease 1:80, 4:86, 4:88
Adenoma 8:79
Adenosine deaminase.
  See ADA deficiency
Adenoviruses 1:78, 8:98
ADH (antidiuretic hormone) 3:3-4, 4:85
Adrenal glands 1:17-18, 3:64
Adrenaline. *See* Epinephrine
African sleeping sickness 6:62, 8:73
Agent Orange 2:42
Agranulocytosis 1:19-20
AIDS (acquired immuno-deficiency syndrome) 1:20-24, 7:69, 7:72, 8:73
  and blood transfusions 1:42, 4:64
  entry through birth canal 1:99
  and gonorrhea 4:25
  history 1:23-24
  HIV testing 1:23

and immune system 4:105, 4:109, 4:110
  as modern pandemic 3:71
  Pneumocystis carinii 1:22, 6:97
AIDS dementia 1:22
Air sac 5:66
Air sickness.
  See Motion sickness
Albinism 1:24-25, 7:97
Alcohol
  and cancer 2:18
  and diarrhea 3:15
  fetal alcohol syndrome 1:26, 3:86-87
  and frostbite 3:105
  nausea from 6:15
Alcoholics Anonymous 1:26, 1:27, 5:94
Alcoholism 1:25-28
  and cirrhosis of liver 2:53
  delirium tremens 1:26, 2:103-4
  dementia 2:106
  Korsakoff's syndrome 1:39
  paranoia 6:59
Alcohol poisoning 1:25
Aldosterone 1:18, 4:84
Allergen(s) 1:28-31, 1:69, 4:39
Allergic purpura 7:20
Allergic rhinitis. *See* Hay fever
Allergies 1:28-31, 1:79, 2:65
  asthma 1:69-72
  food 1:30, 1:31
  hay fever 1:28, 1:29, 2:65, 4:38-42
  and immune system 4:108
  and itching 5:23
  to stings 8:14, 8:16
Alper, Tikva 7:11
Alpha interferon 4:72
ALS (amyotrophic lateral sclerosis) 1:32-34, 1:80
  and Guam disease 4:28-30
Altitude sickness.
  See Polycythemia
Aluminum 4:29
Alveoli 3:57, 5:66
Alveolitis 3:108
Alzheimer's disease 1:34-37, 1:80
  dementia 2:106
Amblyopia 3:78-79

Amebic dysentery 1:13, 3:37, 6:62
Amenorrhea 1:37-38
Amnesia 1:38-39, 2:67
Amniocentesis 2:46
Amniotic fluid 3:88, 7:6
Amphetamines 3:35
Amyotrophic lateral sclerosis.
  See ALS
Anal itching 5:23
Anaphylactic shock 1:31
Anemia(s) 1:40-43, 1:107, 3:85
  aplastic 1:41, 1:42
  pernicious 1:40, 1:41-42, 1:43, 1:80, 8:103
  in pregnancy 7:6-7
  thalassemia 1:41, 8:45-46
  See also Sickle cell anemia
Anencephaly 6:22
Aneurysm 1:43-46, 2:50, 5:21, 8:23
Angina 1:46-47, 2:23
Angiography 1:73, 3:53-54
Angioplasty 1:73
Animal bites 1:51
  snakebites 7:105-8
  spider bites 8:1-3
Animal diseases and humans 1:47-52
  anthrax 1:55-58
  cryptosporidiosis 2:93-94
  Q fever 7:21-22
  rabies 1:48, 1:50, 6:84, 7:22-24
  tularemia 8:77-78
  See also Pets
Animal models 1:49
Ankylosing spondylitis 1:85, 1:87
Anorexia nervosa 1:52-54, 2:7
Anosmia 6:25
Antegrade amnesia 1:38
Anthracosis.
  See Black lung disease
Anthrax 1:49, 1:55-58
Antibiotics
  for gonorrhea 4:23, 4:25
  for infants 5:1
Antibodies 4:107, 5:1
  in rheumatoid arthritis 7:39
Anticoagulants 3:54
Anticonvulsants 3:72-73

Antidiuretic hormone.
  See ADH
Antigens 1:29, 1:79
Antihistamines 4:41
Antiretrovirals 1:22
Antivenin 7:107
Anus 2:69, 7:29
Aorta 1:58, 1:66, 6:70
  coarctation of 2:73
  overriding of 2:73
  transposition of great vessels 2:74
Aortic aneurysm 1:43-45
Aortic stenosis 1:58-59
Aortic valve 1:58
Aphasia 1:59-60
Aplastic anemia 1:41, 1:42
Apnea 2:40, 5:13, 7:98-99
Apocrine glands 3:77
Apoplexy. *See* Stroke
Appendicitis 1:60-62, 3:23, 8:18
Appendicular skeleton 7:88
Appendix 5:40
Apthous ulcer 2:21
Aqueous humor 4:18
Arachnids 6:60-62
Arboviruses 8:73, 8:98
Arenaviruses 8:98
Arrhythmia(s) 1:63-65, 2:74
Arteries 1:66-67, 2:49
  hardening of 4:35-38
  temporal arteritis 8:38-39
Arterioles 2:49
Arthritis. *See* Osteoarthritis; Rheumatoid arthritis
Asbestos 5:16
Asbestosis 3:68
Ascariasis. *See* Roundworms
Ascending colon 5:41
Ashkenazic Jews 4:4, 4:8, 8:36
Aspergillosis 3:108
Asphyxia 1:67-68
  in infants 1:67-68, 2:39-40, 2:41
Aspiration pneumonia 6:98
Aspirin 2:37, 2:68, 2:108
  and embolism 3:54-55
  and hardening of arteries 4:37-38
  and heart problems 4:52
  and Reye's syndrome 7:38
  and roseola 7:48

Redux **6:**32
Reflex sympathetic dystrophy **6:**21
Reflux **5:**33, **5:**36
Reflux esophagitis.
  See Heartburn
Relapsing fevers **7:**30
Renal colic **2:**60, **2:**61, **5:**31
Repetitive strain injuries **2:**24-27
Reproductive system **7:**31-33
Respirator **1:**71
Respiratory distress syndrome **1:**67-68
Respiratory system **7:**33-34
  trachea **5:**44, **6:**24, **8:**65-66
Restless leg syndrome **5:**13
Retina, detached **3:**1-3
Retinitis pigmentosa **7:**35
Retinoblastoma **7:**36
Retinol. *See* Vitamin A
Retrograde amnesia **1:**38
Retroviruses **8:**98
Reye's syndrome **2:**37, **7:**37-38
Rheumatic fever **1:**79, **1:**91, **5:**100, **8:**21-22
Rheumatoid arthritis **1:**80, **1:**81, **1:**83, **7:**39-40
Rh incompatibility **7:**7-8
Rhinoviruses **8:**98
Riboflavin. *See* Vitamin B$_2$
Rickets **6:**40, **7:**41-42, **8:**72
Rickettsiae **1:**88
Rift Valley fever **7:**42-43, **8:**73
Right ventricle **2:**73
Ringing in ears. *See* Tinnitus
Ringworm **3:**107, **6:**82, **7:**43-44
  itching from **5:**24
River blindness **6:**63, **7:**45
RNA (ribonucleic acid) **3:**41
Rocky Mountain spotted fever **1:**91, **7:**45-47, **8:**81
Root, of tooth **8:**37, **8:**38
Root canal **8:**57, **8:**59
Rosacea **1:**14
Roseola **7:**48
Rotaviruses **3:**14
Roundworms **6:**63, **6:**81, **7:**49
Rous, Peyton **8:**98
Rubella.
  See "German" measles
Rubeola. *See* Measles
Ruptured disk.
  See Slipped/ruptured disk

S

Sabin, Albert **6:**107
Saccular aneurysm **1:**44
Saccule **1:**92

SAD. *See* Seasonal affective disorder
Safe sex **1:**22-23, **7:**71
St. Anthony's fire **7:**96
Salivary glands **3:**22, **3:**77, **7:**50
Salk, Jonas **6:**107
Salmonella **3:**94, **6:**65, **7:**51-52
Sandfly fever **6:**62
Sarcoidosis **7:**52-53
Sarcoma **8:**98
Saturated fat **3:**18
Scabies **6:**61, **7:**53-54
Scalds **2:**9-12
Scalp
  dandruff **5:**23, **7:**66
  ringworm **7:**44
Scarlet fever **5:**28-29, **7:**54-55, **8:**22
Schick test **3:**26
Schistosomiasis **6:**63, **7:**55-57, **8:**73
Schizophrenia **1:**75, **5:**109, **6:**58, **7:**57-59
Sciatica **1:**85, **7:**59-60, **7:**100
SCID (severe combined immunity deficiency) **4:**108, **6:**85, **7:**60-61
Scleroderma **1:**80, **1:**81, **5:**16, **7:**61-62
Scoliosis **1:**85, **7:**62-63
Scrapie **1:**49, **5:**37, **7:**11
Scrub typhus **8:**82
Scurvy **7:**63-64
Seasickness **7:**64-65
Seasonal affective disorder (SAD) **6:**89, **7:**65-66
Seborrhea **7:**66-67, **7:**95
Seborrheic keratoses **7:**97
Sebum **1:**14, **1:**15, **1:**101
Secretin **4:**85
Seizure. *See* Convulsion
Selenium **3:**21
Semen **7:**32
Semicircular canals **1:**92
Semmelweis, Ignaz **7:**18
Senile cataract **2:**28
Senile purpura **7:**20
Senses **7:**67-68
Sensorineural hearing loss **2:**99, **2:**101
Sensory hearing loss **2:**99, **2:**100
Septal defects **2:**72, **2:**74
Septicemia.
  See Blood poisoning
Septum **6:**25
Serotonin **1:**98, **5:**95
Serum **1:**106
Severe combined immunity deficiency. *See* SCID

Sex
  and cancer **2:**19
  impotence **4:**110-11
  See also Sexually transmitted diseases
Sex-chromosome abnormalities **2:**45, **2:**46
Sex hormones **4:**88
Sexually transmitted diseases **7:**68-72
  chlamydia **1:**90, **7:**70, **7:**71, **7:**72
  entry through birth canal **1:**99
  genital herpes **4:**10-13
  gonorrhea **1:**90, **3:**83, **4:**22-25
  pelvic inflammatory disease **3:**83, **4:**23, **6:**50, **6:**73
  safe sex **1:**22-23, **7:**71
  syphilis **1:**51, **1:**91, **1:**99, **7:**72, **8:**29-31
  trichomonas **6:**62, **7:**72, **8:**69-70
  See also AIDS
Shared paranoid disorder **6:**59
Shark cartilage **2:**27
Shellfish **3:**94-95
Shigellosis **3:**37, **3:**42
Shingles **2:**35, **2:**36, **2:**38, **7:**72-74
  itching from **5:**24
  and neuralgia **6:**21
Shin splints **3:**103
Shock **7:**74-76
Shock treatment.
  See Electroconvulsive therapy
Shoes **1:**75, **1:**105, **3:**97
Shortness of breath **3:**58
Short stature **4:**86, **7:**76-77, **8:**48
Shoulder, bursitis in **2:**12-13
Sickle cell anemia **1:**41, **5:**77, **7:**77-80
Siderosis **3:**68, **7:**80-81
SIDS (sudden infant death syndrome) **7:**81-83
Sight. *See* Eyes and vision
Sigmoid colon **5:**41
Sigmoidoscopy **3:**27
Silicone **3:**67
Silicosis **3:**68, **7:**83-84
Silver amalgam **2:**111
Silver nitrate **4:**24
Sinemet **6:**68
Sinuses **6:**24
Sinusitis **6:**25, **7:**84-86
Sinus node **1:**63
Sjögren's syndrome **1:**80

Skeletal muscles **6:**4, **7:**86-87
Skeleton **2:**1, **7:**88
Skin **7:**90-91
Skin diseases/disorders **5:**24, **7:**94-98
  acne **1:**14-15
  bacterial and viral **7:**96
  cancer **7:**91-94, **8:**27
  contact dermatitis **6:**104, **7:**26
  discoloration **7:**97
  eczema **3:**46-47, **7:**27, **7:**95
  fungal **7:**96-97
  growths **7:**98
  psoriasis **1:**80, **1:**81, **7:**16-17
  seborrhea **7:**66-67
  See also Rashes
Skull **2:**5
SLE. *See* Systemic lupus erythematosus
Sleep
  apnea **5:**13, **7:**98-99
  insomnia **5:**12-15
  narcolepsy **5:**13, **6:**13-14
  and sudden infant death syndrome **7:**82-83
Sleeping pills **5:**13-14
Sleeping sickness **6:**62, **8:**73
Slipped/ruptured disk **1:**84, **1:**85, **7:**59, **7:**99-101
Slit lamp **4:**19
Slow viruses. *See* Prions and slow viruses
Small intestine **3:**22, **7:**101-2
  Crohn's disease **2:**86-89
  gastroenteritis **3:**23, **4:**3-4
Smallpox **1:**50, **1:**51, **7:**102-3, **8:**88
Smell **6:**25, **7:**67
Smoking
  and cancer **2:**18, **8:**54
  and emphysema **3:**56, **3:**57-58, **3:**59
  and pregnancy **8:**54
  quitting **8:**53
Smooth muscles **7:**104
Snakebites **7:**105-8
Sneezing **7:**108-9
Sodium **3:**21, **3:**38
Sore throat **7:**109-11
  See also "Strep"
Space sickness **5:**105
Spasm **7:**111-12
  smooth muscle **7:**104-5
  tic **8:**48-49
Spastic cerebral palsy **2:**32-33
Speech. *See* Aphasia
Sphincter muscles **4:**53, **7:**29
Spider bites **8:**1-3
Spina bifida **6:**21-22, **8:**4-6
Spina bifida occulta **8:**4